THE MAUDSLEY

Maudsley Monographs

MAUDSLEY MONOGRAPHS

HENRY MAUDSLEY, from whom the series of monographs takes its name, was the founder of The Maudsley Hospital and the most prominent English psychiatrist of his generation. The Maudsley Hospital was united with the Bethlem Royal Hospital in 1948 and its medical school, renamed the Institute of Psychiatry at the same time, became a constituent part of the British Postgraduate Medical Federation. It is now associated with King's College, London, and entrusted with the duty of advancing psychiatry by teaching and research. The Bethlem-Maudsley NHS Trust, together with the Institute of Psychiatry, are jointly known as The Maudsley.

The monograph series reports work carried out at The Maudsley. Some of the monographs are directly concerned with clinical problems; others, less obviously relevant, are in scientific fields that are cultivated for the furtherance of psychiatry.

Editor
Professor David P Goldberg MA DM MSc FRCP FRCPsych DPM
Assistant Editors
Dr A S David MPhil MSc FRCP MRCPsych MD
Dr T Wykes BSc PhD MPhil

Previous Editors

1955-1962	Professor Sir Aubrey Lewis LLD DSc MD FRCP and Professor G W Harris MA MD DSc FRS
1962-1966	Professor Sir Aubrey Lewis LLD DSc MD FRCP
1966-1970	Professor Sir Denis Hill MB FRCP FRCPsych DPM and Professor J T Eayrs PhD DSc
1970-1979	Professor Sir Denis Hill MB FRCP FRCPsych DPM and Professor G S Brindley MD FRCP FRS
1979-1981	Professor G S Brindley MD FRCP FRS and Professor G F M Russell MD FRCP FRCP(ED) FRCPsych
1981-1983	Professor G F M Russell MD FRCP FRCP(ED) FRCPsych
1983-1989	Professor G F M Russell MD FRCP FRCP(ED) FRCPsych and Professor E Marley MA MD DSc FRCP FRCPsych DPM
1989-1993	Professor G F M Russell MD FRCP FRCP(ED) FRCPsych and Professor B H Anderton BSc PhD

Maudsley Monographs number thirty-seven

Compliance with Treatment in Schizophrenia

Alec Buchanan
Institute of Psychiatry, London

a member of the Taylor & Francis group

Reprinted 2000

Psychology Press Ltd, Publishers
27 Church Road
Hove
East Sussex, BN3 2FA
UK

http://www.psypress.co.uk

ISBN 1-84169-254-9 (JANSSEN-CILAG gratis edition)
(Sold by the publisher Psychology Press Ltd
under the following ISBN 0-86377-422-9)
ISSN 0076-5465

British Library Cataloguing-in-Publication Data
A catalogue record for this book is available from the British Library

Printed and bound in the UK by TJ International Ltd, Padstow, Cornwall.

To James and Elizabeth

Contents

Acknowledgments

Many people have contributed, some knowingly, to the ideas presented here. I can identify some. Principle among these are my colleagues at the Bethlem and Maudsley Hospital and the Institute of Psychiatry. Professors Gerald Russell, Stephen Hirsch and Richard Mindham examined the thesis on which much of this book is based and their comments have been incorporated. The thesis was supervised by Dr. John Cutting. Statistical advice was provided by Dr. Graham Dunn and Mrs. Katarzyna Ray of the Biometrics Department at the Institute of Psychiatry. Computing advice was provided by Dr. Graham Robertson and Dr. Don Grubin.

Abstract

There is a myth that people with mental disorders comply poorly with treatment. In fact, psychiatric patients are no more likely than patients in other medical specialities to go against the advice of their doctor. That said, it is easy to find instances where psychotropic medication is refused by the supposed beneficiary. The value of neuroleptic treatment in schizophrenia is now widely accepted. Failure to take such treatment is associated with relapse, and relapse may endanger the patient and other people. Despite this, people with schizophrenia frequently fail to take their treatment. This study shows that one-third can be expected to be noncompliant within two years of leaving a general adult psychiatry ward. The research was designed to examine the reasons why.

A good deal was known before the study was undertaken. Factors that had been linked to poor compliance included low socioeconomic status, an unstable lifestyle, and a generally negative attitude to one's predicament. Factors that helped to improve adherence had been found to include keeping the drug regimen simple, persuading the patient to take the medication in depot, rather than oral, form, and minimising side-effects, especially akathisia. These findings were confirmed with two exceptions. First, the form in which medication was taken made no difference. Second, the side effect that reduced compliance was akinesia rather than akathisia. If replicated, this is an encouraging finding. Akinesia is more easily remedied.

Some issues addressed here, however, have not received widespread attention previously. Insight, usually defined as a recognition that one is ill, has usually been held to improve compliance but the literature is inconsistent. This study shows that it depends what is meant by insight. Abstract, even philosophical enquiries as to whether or not people regard themselves as ill are of no assistance in predicting whether or not they will take their treatment. Specific questions regarding medication, however, are of value. This study showed that by asking patients whether treatment had helped previously, doctors can predict compliance to some extent. The study also demonstrates the value of asking patients directly about their intentions, a point that had not been made elsewhere. Finally, the study confirms what might have been predicted but had not been shown previously: The patients whose compliance warrants particular attention are those who have stopped taking their medication in the past.

CHAPTER ONE

Literature review

INTRODUCTION

The degree to which patients comply with the advice of health workers is of importance in clinical practice, where the health of the patient is directly affected, and in research, where drug trials in particular depend on adherence to medical instructions. Blackwell (1976) has argued that an increasing interest in compliance among doctors and the general public reflects a decrease in professional paternalism, greater concern for patients' rights, and a growing emphasis on preventive health care and hence on long-term prophylactic and maintenance treatments. The value of neuroleptic maintenance treatment in schizophrenia is now generally accepted. This chapter reviews the factors that have been associated with compliance in this context.

Surveys of general medical populations have concluded that roughly one-third of patients can be expected to fail to comply with treatment (Davis, 1966). There is a great deal of variation in reported default rates, however, and this is equally the case when psychiatric populations are studied. Reviewing the literature with regard to out-patient psychiatric services, Baekeland and Lundwall (1975) found that between 20 and 57% of patients failed to return after their first visit. Among schizophrenic out-patients, Van Putten (1974) concluded that between 24 and 63% of patients failed to take the correct drug in the correct dosage. Renton, Affleck, Carstairs, and Forrest (1963) followed up 132 schizophrenics one year after discharge and found that 46% failed to take their neuroleptics as instructed. Similar figures have been recorded in schizophrenic populations by Parkes, Brown, and Monck (1962) and more recently by Bartko, Herczeg, and Zador (1988).

Some of these studies refer to compliance with medication regimens, others to attendance at out-patient clinics. The term "compliance" has also been used with reference to the promptness with which a patient seeks care, the degree to which he or she adheres to other medical instructions and his or her willingness to remain in hospital after admission. The different levels of compliance associated with each of these contribute to the inconsistencies in reported compliance rates. Little evidence exists, however, demonstrating that variables associated with compliance affect one outcome measure more than another. For this reason reference will be made to research that uses various measures where the findings are of relevance to the definition provided by Haynes (1979), that is, that compliance is the extent to which a person's behaviour coincides with medical or health worker advice. Blackwell (1976) uses a similar definition but prefers the term "adherence"; this will be used synonymously. Compliance with taking medication can be measured by direct or indirect methods. Direct methods include the measurement of blood levels and the analysis of urine for drugs, markers, or metabolites. While preferable in most respects, this form of measurement presents several problems. It is relatively inconvenient and may be expensive. Pharmacokinetic variability may make it difficult to establish a blood or urinary drug concentration at which a patient can be said to be compliant. Finally, consent may be more difficult to obtain, particularly from noncompliant patients. Indirect methods include using the impression of the treating physician, interviewing patients, counting the number of tablets remaining in a patient's supply, and measuring therapeutic outcome. The last of these requires a reliably identifiable result of treatment and has not been widely used in psychiatric populations. The others are all subject to the warning of Hippocrates, that patients often lie when they state that they have taken certain medicines. Gordis, Markovitz, and Lilienfeld (1969) found a marked discrepancy between compliance assessed at interview and that confirmed by urine analysis. Bergman and Werner (1963) found a similar discrepancy when they compared pill counts with urine tests. Nor are indirect methods consistent with each other. Park and Lipman (1964) found marked differences between compliance assessed at interview and that measured by pill counts. Perhaps most disturbingly, Gordis (1979), in his review, concludes that doctors are poor judges of the compliance of their patients, usually erring on the side of optimism. Indirect measures of compliance are more common in the literature, probably because they are easier to use, but where possible reference will be made to direct methods.

To a great extent, people with schizophrenia comply well or poorly for reasons similar to those of other patients. For this reason, where the literature allows, each section of this chapter starts with an overview of compliance in general medical populations before the focus narrows to examine psychiatric populations in general and schizophrenia in particular

PATIENT CHARACTERISTICS: SOCIODEMOGRAPHIC

Age

Numerous studies have examined the effects of age on compliance; the findings are inconsistent. In the field of general practice, Waters, Gould, and Lunn (1976) found that 7% of prescriptions issued were never presented at a chemist. They found that the 25–34 age group were least likely to present their prescriptions whereas older patients complied better. West, Graham, Swanson, and Wilkinson (1977) undertook a five-year follow-up study of 800 attenders at an anti-smoking clinic and also found that older patients were more likely to comply with treatment. Different conclusions were reached by Quinn, Federspiel, Lefkowitz, and Christie (1977) who followed up 311 patients who acquired rheumatic fever in Nashville, Tennessee, between 1963 and 1969 and measured their adherence to penicillin prophylaxis. The authors found that only 53% of their sample took their treatment regularly and that younger patients were more likely to comply, observing, somewhat curiously, that "younger persons are less autonomous in their ideas". The inconsistency of reports in this area reflects the variation in the populations under study. In the mining community described by Waters et al. (1976), the 25–34 age group contained a large number of young men for whom the object of medical consultation was to "obtain a medical certificate to entitle them to sickness benefit". Older patients were more likely to attend requesting medication and this is reflected in their compliance. In the Nashville study, as the authors propose, it seems likely that the improved compliance among younger patients is related to the higher rate of recurrence in this group. Reviewing the literature, Haynes, Taylor, and Sacket (1979) found no consistent relationship between age and compliance. The majority of studies in this area draw conclusions similar to those of Prickman et al. (1958) who reviewed the records of 231 employees of a large corporation, each of whom had undergone at least two examinations at the Mayo clinic. They found no correlation between an employee's age and the degree to which he or she complied with medical advice.

A similar picture emerges with regard to psychiatric treatment. Baekeland and Lundwall (1975), reviewing the literature, looked at 51 studies, of which 35 (68.6%) found age to be unrelated to dropping out of treatment. Turner, Gardner, and Higgins (1970) looked at 338 cases drawn from a psychiatric case register in New York State and found no differences in age distribution between the group lost to follow-up and the rest of their sample. Rae (1972) undertook a two-year follow-up of 58 alcoholic in-patients and found no correlation between prognosis and age. Where a difference between age groups has been identified, the conclusion has usually been that older patients comply better. Myers (1975) found a significant association ($P < 0.001$) between increasing age and continued attendance at a general hospital psychiatric out-patient department. Davis, Estess, Simonton, and Gonda (1977), also looking at an out-patient population, found that 58% of patients under 40 terminated treatment compared with only 37% of the over-forties. Raynes and Patch (1971) reviewed the records of 237 consecutive psychiatric admissions. They found that the average age of their sample was 36.5 years, whereas that of patients discharged against medical advice was 32.6 years and that of patients going "absent without leave" was 32.4 years. The effect of age has not been studied with respect to exclusively schizophrenic patient populations.

Sex
The sex of a patient has not been found consistently to affect the likelihood of compliance with treatment. Davis (1968a,b) studied 154 patients at a general medical out-patient clinic and found no difference between men and women in the extent to which they followed medical advice. Even when differences have been found, these are often trivial. Hurtado, Greenlick, and Colombo (1973), looking at appointment failures in a multi-speciality group practice in the United States found that men missed their appointments 17.2% of the time, whereas the corresponding figure for women was 15.7%. In certain specialised samples significant differences have been found. Kanzler, Jaffe, and Zeidenberg (1976) undertook a four-year follow up of "graduates" of an anti-smoking programme. They found that 57% of males were still smoking as compared with 30% of females.

In psychiatric populations sex differences have also been noted in specific populations. Craig, Huffine, and Brooks (1974), looking at a relatively deprived inner-city population in Baltimore, found that males were less likely to progress successfully from referral by the emergency service to regular out-patient attendance, and report the finding of

Brody, Derbyshire, and Schliefer (1967) that when males do enter treatment they do so under less favourable circumstances, for instance, through the courts. A later study of the same population (Craig & Huffine, 1976), however, showed that once patients entered treatment the drop-out rates were the same for males and females. In Britain, Caine and Wijesinghe (1976) used a sample drawn from 100 patients referred to a psychotherapy clinic and found no significant differences in age or sex between treatment responders and those who dropped out of therapy. Despite the lack of research in this area, it seems likely that the situation is similar in schizophrenia.

Socioeconomic status

An association between low socioeconomic status and poor compliance has long been recognised. Hardy (1948) described such an association among medical patients and Gray, Kesler, and Moody (1966) recorded similar findings when they studied the effects of social class on oral polio vaccine uptake. In psychiatric populations similar findings have been recorded with regard to compliance with neuroleptic medication (Winkelman, 1964), out-patient psychotherapy (Winder & Hersko, 1955), out-patient child psychiatry (Lefebvre, Sommerauer, Cohen, Waldron, & Perry, 1983), alcoholism (Baekeland, Lundwall, & Shanahan, 1973; Pisani & Motansky, 1970) and drug addiction (Rosenberg, Davidson, & Patch, 1972).

Social stability

Studies of patient compliance have examined social stability in the areas of marriage, occupation, and, to a lesser extent, residence. Being married has been found to be associated with good compliance in a study of 66 consecutive discharges from a tuberculosis hospital (Pragoff, 1962) and in a long-term prospective study of the effects of dietary modification on the incidence of coronary artery disease (Archer, Rinzler, & Christakis, 1967). A study of 178 elderly chronically ill reached similar conclusions (Schwartz, Wang, Zeitz, & Goss, 1962). A stable "social milieu", in the form of a supportive spouse, has been reported as associated with good compliance at a smoker's clinic (West et al., 1977). Stable employment was found to be associated with compliance by Pragoff (1962) and higher social class with regular dental attendance by Nikias (1968). Reports in this area are inconsistent, however. Being married was not associated with good compliance in a study of 290 consecutive discharges from a general hospital in Canada (Brand, Smith, & Brand, 1977) and occupational status was not linked to dietary compliance in Archer et al.'s (1967) study of coronary artery disease.

Among psychiatric patients there is evidence that the less socially stable are more likely to drop out of treatment. Altman, Angle, Brown, and Sletten (1972a) undertook a multivariate analysis of the demographic and diagnostic details of 3383 psychiatric in-patients and found that patients who were single and not earning a salary were more likely to, in the authors' word, "elope". A study of 511 heroin addicts in New York (Perkins & Bloch, 1971) showed that the level of drug use was highest among those who were unemployed and not self-supporting and a recent British study has shown that the children of parents who are separated are more likely to drop out of treatment (Cottrell, Hill, Walk, Dearnaley, & Ierotheou, 1988). In their review of the literature Baekeland and Lundwall (1975) conclude that, among psychiatric populations, the less socially stable a patient is, the more likely he or she is to drop out of treatment. Occupational and residential stability seem to carry more weight than marital stability, and occupational stability is a more potent predictor of dropping out in alcoholics and drug addicts than in other groups of psychiatric patients.

Family attitudes

The attitudes of a patient's family would seem likely to affect substantially his or her compliance but this is not an area that has been widely studied. Working from a sociological perspective, Davis (1967) argued that the prediction of compliance involved the identification of the patient's social norms, norms that will be heavily influenced by the attitudes of a patient's family. Heinzelmann and Bagley (1970), as part of a larger project investigating the effect of physical activity on cardiovascular risk, investigated adherence to medical advice and found that it was substantially affected by the attitude of the patient's spouse.

In the psychiatric field, the work of Vaughn and Leff (1976) describing the increased risk of relapse in schizophrenics living with high "expressed emotion" families is well known. It has not been suggested, however, that failed compliance with anti-psychotic medication is the mediating factor in relapse. Parkes et al. (1962) drew attention to the vital role of relatives in the supervision of schizophrenics in the community. Willcox, Gillan, and Hare (1965), examining the drug compliance of 125 psychiatric out-patients, found that men living with their wives defaulted less often and reflected that this demonstrated the beneficial aspects of supervision. It may also be that patients living with their wives represented a less chaotic group of patients who were more motivated to comply for various other reasons. Family attitudes have also been investigated in child psychiatry, where they affect compliance with treatment almost by definition (e.g. Ross & Lacey, 1961).

PATIENT CHARACTERISTICS: PSYCHOLOGICAL

This section will review the various personality characteristics and attitudes that have been linked to poor compliance. In this area the problems noted previously, of study groups, variables under investigation, and compliance outcome measures that vary from paper to paper, are compounded by the presence of several different conceptual frameworks that different workers use to explain their results. This section will examine first the general characteristics that have been linked to poor compliance, and will then review the more specific attitudes with regard to illness exhibited by patients who fail to take their medication.

General

The psychological characteristics of patients who fail to comply have not been widely studied in the general patient population. Lewis, Lorenz, and Calden (1955) reviewed 100 consecutive discharges against medical advice from a tuberculosis hospital. They found that, compared with a control group who had been discharged in the normal way, patients who had discharged themselves had an "impaired capacity to develop interpersonal attachments". The subject has been more widely examined in psychiatric populations. In the field of psychoanalysis there is a large body of literature concerning the lack of "psychological mindedness" of patients who fail to comply (e.g. Brown & Kosterlitz, 1964). So-called sociopathic traits have been widely linked to poor compliance. Greenwald and Bartemeier (1963) looked at 191 discharges from a private hospital in the United States; a somewhat startling 35% of these took place against medical advice. The authors found that 7% of patients discharging themselves had a diagnosis of sociopathic personality compared with 3% of patients discharged in the normal way. Altman et al. (1972a) identify three characteristics of patients who leave hospital of their own accord as impulsivity, a disregard for rules and regulations, and a tendency to act out under stress. Hiler (1959) found that patients who terminated treatment early were more likely to complain of getting into trouble or of "paranoid or schizoid feelings". Hostility has also been linked to poor compliance. Wilkinson, Prado, Williams, and Schnadt (1971) looked at 132 patients entering a 90-day alcohol treatment programme. They found that those who failed to complete were more hostile and aggressive, more anxious, and more "confused and disturbed in their thinking". Other authors have examined more exotic aspects of patient's personalities. Thus Orford (1974) identified "simplistic thinking" as associated with early treatment failure in alcoholism. Voth (1965) linked treatment failure to a variable termed "autokinesis", defined in patients as a tendency towards greater autonomy, a relative independence of environmental stimuli, being hard to get to know, and tending not to form close relationships quickly. One methodological failing of all of these studies is the unreliability of the personality criteria used. Terms such as "aggressive", "confused", and "disturbed" do not lend themselves to operational definition and the problem is compounded by the pejorative connotation of terms such as "sociopathic" and "simplistic".

Specific
The specific attitudes and behaviours of patients with regard to psychological illness and the consequences for treatment adherence will be examined first with regard to the patient's attitude to illness in general and his own illness, and then with regard to his attitude to treatment in general and his own treatment. Some authors have attempted to develop models that explain various combinations of these attitudes; these models will be reviewed in conclusion.

Attitudes to illness in general
Much of the work in this area comes from the general medical literature. Becker, Drachman, and Kirscht (1974), interviewing the mothers of 125 children being treated with antibiotics for otitis media, found that mothers who complied with various aspects of the regimen were more interested in many diverse aspects of their child's health than were mothers who complied poorly. Davis (1967) assessed the attitudes of 397 Indiana farmers and then measured their compliance with medical advice. He found that patients with low compliance were more likely to endorse statements such as "if you wait long enough you can get over any illness", "some old-fashioned remedies are still better than things you buy at the drugstore", and "illness and trouble is one way God shows his displeasure". Blackwell (1976), in his review of the literature, reflects that "every individual's behavior in relation to health and illness is determined by such personal and culturally endorsed belief systems".

Fiester, Mahrer, and Giambra (1974) studied 513 patients attending a psychiatric out-patient department. They concluded that patients who dropped out of treatment differed from others only in the number of times they had done the same thing previously, and claimed that there existed "a class of persons who want what typical mental health facilities do not provide, who do not seek what these facilities do offer". The dangers of such generalisations have also been pointed out; Wooley and Blackwell (1975) argued that appearing angry towards the therapist may be a means by which patients sustain the attention and concern of their doctor. This view gains some support from the work of Richards (1964) who studied 233 patients, the entire in-patient population, in a public psychiatric hospital in the United States. He found that drug refusers differed from other patients in holding a less favourable view of life outside hospital. In this respect they resembled the group of patients identified by Gordon and Groth (1961) as "stayers", patients whose low opinion of life at home led them to tell staff that they did not want to leave.

Attitudes of patients to their own illness

Patients are more likely to adhere to treatment regimens if they accept that they are ill. A lack of such acceptance invokes elements such as denial and lack of insight; these will be examined first. Once patients accept that they are ill their compliance will be subject to numerous other psychological factors; these will be examined later.

Denial of illness has been linked to poor compliance. Mozdzierz, Macchitelli, Conway, and Krauss (1973) compared the personality characteristics of 22 alcoholics who left hospital against medical advice with those of controls, matched for educational and marital status, who had been discharged in the normal way. They found that those discharged against advice had higher scores on measures of denial and defensiveness. Nelson and Hoffmann (1972) recorded similar findings, also among alcoholics. A familiar and related phenomenon is that described by Bursten (1985), whose patient accepted that he suffered from depression but refused to take prophylactic medication because he saw the cause of his illness as psychological. The term "denial" is not widely used outside the psychoanalytic literature in describing the views of psychotic patients. Most clinicians would use the term insight in referring to the attitudes of such patients to their symptoms.

In any discussion of the role of insight the first question to be dealt with is whether loss of insight is simply a reflection of other aspects of the patient's illness. It would seem that this is not the case. McEvoy et al. (1989) studied the levels of insight and general psychopathology of 52 patients, all diagnosed as schizophrenic using DSM-III criteria (American Psychiatric Association, 1980). All were suffering a relapse of their psychosis. The authors found no consistent relationship between the levels of psychopathology and insight over time. Heinrichs, Cohen, and Carpenter (1985) recorded similar findings in a sample of 39 patients diagnosed using RDC criteria (Spitzer, Endicott, Gibson, & Robins 1978). Several authors have linked lack of insight to poor compliance. The study of McEvoy et al. (1989) found the two to be "moderately correlated". Lin, Spiga, and Fortsch (1979) assessed the insight and compliance of 100 schizophrenics. Of 31 patients with good insight, 17 failed to comply with medication whereas of 69 patients with poor insight, 57 failed to comply. Nelson (1975), Marder et al. (1983), and Bartko et al. (1988) have recorded similar findings.

Once a patient has accepted that he or she suffers from an illness that patient's treatment adherence is affected by numerous psychological factors. Compliance has been found to be correlated with perceived seriousness of illness in general medical populations (Francis, Korsch, & Morris, 1969) and poor treatment adherence has been attributed to the stigma of incurable mental illness in a group of patients receiving lithium prophylaxis (Prien & Caffey, 1977). It seems likely that similar factors apply to patients receiving maintenance treatment for schizophrenia. Among psychiatric populations, one of the most detailed studies is also one of the most methodologically flawed. Soskis and Bowers (1969) interviewed 32 schizophrenics three to seven years after their discharges from hospital. Patients who failed to comply were not interviewed. The authors found that attitudes such as "in a way, my illness helped me grow up" and "although it may not put them in the hospital, most people have an experience like I had at some point in their life" were associated with improved social adjustment and a lower rate of re-hospitalisation. Although these attitudes are described in detail, the authors do not exclude the possibility that they are the result rather than the cause of good levels of adjustment. This study was partially replicated by McGlashan and Carpenter (1981) who used the same attitude scale to interview 30 schizophrenics one year after discharge and found that those who were less negative about their illness had better outcomes according to social and psychopathological criteria. Other authors have investigated the positive features of remaining ill. Havens (1968) has argued that psychotic symptoms benefit patients by providing them with "attention-getting mechanisms", thereby producing "secondary gain". Catatonic symptoms provide a means for the patient to escape "psychotic character adjustment" and the patient is in fact less ill when he is floridly psychotic. Little evidence has emerged subsequently in support of this view, although in the isolated instance of grandiosity there is a suggestion that patients may prefer the symptoms to the treatment. Bartko et al (1988) studied 58 schizophrenics, rating insight, compliance, and psychopathology, and found that poor insight and grandiosity were particularly associated with poor compliance.

Attitude to treatment in general

Attitudes to treatment in general have been linked to compliance in both general and psychiatric populations. Suchman (1967) interviewed 115 workers in the sugar cane industry in Puerto Rico and assessed their subsequent compliance with preventive health measures. Predictably, he found that those who indicated a greater awareness of the value of such measures complied better. Attitudes to treatment associated with poor compliance in psychiatric populations include "you only take a medicine when you're ill and not when you're better" and "you should give the body a rest from time to time" (Stimson, 1974). Johnson (1974) interviewed over 300 patients receiving antidepressant medication in general practice and out-patient settings. He found that two particular attitudes on the part of patients were associated with poor compliance, namely, a feeling of guilt at having to rely on drugs and a fear of developing dependence.

Attitude of patients to their own treatment

Geersten, Gray, and Ward (1973) interviewed 123 patients with rheumatoid arthritis and then followed their progress in an out-patient clinic. Predictably, they found an association between poor compliance and a lack of faith in the specific form of treatment that the patient was being offered. The importance of similar factors in psychiatric populations was emphasised by Hogan, Awad, and Eastwood (1983) who tested a self-report scale predictive of drug compliance in a group of schizophrenic patients. Discriminant and factor analysis demonstrated that the maximum variability in responses was accounted for by items reflecting how the patient felt about medication rather than what he or she knew about the treatment regime. This view is supported by the work of Michaux (1961) who undertook a double-blind clinical trial of chlorpromazine using an out-patient psychiatric population. Deviations from the prescribed regimen were found to be significantly correlated with "emotional resistance" to drug treatment. Richards' (1964) sample of 233 psychiatric in-patients rated "medicine" less favourably than their more compliant peers. Lin et al. (1979) interviewed 100 in-patient schizophrenics and assessed the degree of benefit that they perceived in taking medication. Of 49 patients who perceived benefit, 18 complied with medication, whereas of 51 patients who perceived no benefit, only 8 complied. It is also clear that the views of patients with regard to their treatment change over time. Stimson (1974) emphasised this in his review of patient attitudes and Seeman (1974) described sequential changes in the attitudes to treatment of schizophrenics in psychotherapy. Finally, Freedman et al. (1958), examining the doctor–patient relationship, showed that patients whose expectations were fulfilled were more likely to continue with treatment. This finding begs the questions of what these expectations comprised and in what ways those of patients who complied poorly remained unfulfilled.

Models of compliance

The review of demographic factors associated with poor compliance demonstrated that these varied across different treatment settings and patient groups. It is evident that the same is true of patients' attitudes. It is also evident that demographic factors and patients' attitudes, taken in isolation, provide little information as to how patients come to their decisions. For these reasons several authors have sought to develop models that include many of the factors discussed earlier and that seek to elucidate the mechanisms by which patients make their decisions about health care.

The oldest of these is the Health Belief Model (Rosenstock, 1966). It was proposed that behaviour related to one's own health was determined by three factors, namely, the perceived benefits of acting, specific cues to acting (for instance, symptoms and social pressure), and the "readiness" of the individual to act. "Readiness" in turn was composed of the perceived seriousness of the illness in question and the individual's susceptibility. The model was originally designed to explain preventative health behaviour such as adhering to a diet or stopping smoking but has since been expanded to explain compliance with prescribed medication. Becker and Maiman (1975) developed the model to include "modifying" and "enabling" factors such as general faith in physicians and the complexity of treatment regimens, and various authors have claimed validity for the model in different patient groups (see Becker et al., 1977). Related to the Health Belief Model is the Theory of Reasoned Action (Ried & Christensen, 1988), which differentiates between behavioural intention and behaviour: What we intend to do may not be what actually happens. Feather (1959) proposed a model for patients' decision-making based on "attainment attractiveness", "choice potential", and "success probability", emphasising the importance of past learning experiences. Finally, Leventhal (1971) has described a "parallel response model" to explain the behaviour of a person who realises that he or she is ill. Two responses occur simultaneously or consecutively, one consisting of "danger control" and the other of "fear control". "Danger control" responses are generally appropriate, whereas "fear control" responses lead to poor treatment adherence and are promoted by such factors as ambiguity in medical advice and poor health education. At their simplest, these models seem to state the obvious, whereas attempts to include more variables (e.g. Becker & Maiman, 1975) generally deprive them of some of their explanatory power when it becomes clear that some of these variables interact with each other and affect compliance in a way not covered by the model. Nevertheless, they do offer a means of assessing various associations with compliance that are otherwise of doubtful significance and the prospect of systematically designed intervention strategies. They await evaluation in well-designed prospective studies.

A somewhat different emphasis is adopted by Mechanic and Volkart (1961) who are concerned with the various filters that exist between developing symptoms and attending for medical care. They develop the concept of the "sick role" as described by Parsons (1982), a group of behaviours to which persons "escape" when permitted to do so by their doctor, their intimates, or others who have influence on them. A patient will only attend for treatment if his or her complaints are regarded by doctor and relatives as symptoms of illness. Although this is important in the understanding of health-seeking behaviour in general, the implications for the management of individual patients are less clear.

EDUCATION AND INFORMATION

There is an extensive literature purporting to show that patient compliance can be improved with appropriate education. Blackwell (1976) quotes the improvements in compliance consequent on educational supervision by nurses and pharmacists in patients with hypertension, and Cohen and Richardson (1970) found that "gross ignorance" was linked with attrition from a child guidance clinic (although with a low level of statistical significance, $P < 0.1$). Falloon (1984) has argued for the crucial role of education in achieving good treatment adherence in schizophrenic patients. Research also exists pertaining to the related subject of information retention. Ley and Spelman (1965) found that their sample of medical out-patient attenders had forgotten one-third of what their consultant told them by the time they left the consulting room, and Joyce, Caple, Mason, Reynolds, and Mathews (1969) found that 54 patients at a rheumatology clinic remembered only half of what they had been told. The degree to which information was retained was influenced by its type and quantity (Ley & Spelman, 1965) as well as by the patient's preconceptions (Joyce et al., 1969). Although the value of patient education in improving compliance is assumed by many authors, much of the research in this area is methodologically weak and the evidence equivocal. Hagan, Beck, Kunce, and Heiser (1983) showed an educational videotape to a group of patients being discharged from a psychiatric hospital. They found that patients who had watched the video were more likely to attend for their first out-patient appointment. The authors did not measure the patients' levels of knowledge about their illness, however, and consequently it is not clear that this was the cause of the improved attendance. The literature has been reviewed by Ley and Morris (1984). The authors identified 32 studies that showed an increase in patients' levels of knowledge and in 16 of these the effect on compliance had been noted. Eight studies showed that compliance improved with greater knowledge whereas the other eight showed no change.

The lack of hard evidence has led Meichenbaum and Turk (1987) to conclude:

> there appears to be minimal association between the amount of information patients have about their illness and adherence. The problem of nonadherence is rarely one of lack of knowledge.

This view, expressed in reference to patient populations in general, has been echoed with respect to a schizophrenic sample by Nelson (1975) and is lent further support by the work of Soskis (1978) who used a structured interview to assess the levels of knowledge of 25 schizophrenics and 25 medical in-patient controls. Schizophrenics were better informed than controls with regard to the side-effects and risks of medication but when asked if, given the choice, they would take medication, only 56% of schizophrenics said they would do so as compared with 93% of controls. This study did not, however, control for severity of illness and the benefits of medication. Hogan et al. (1983) were able to consign 89% of their schizophrenic sample to compliant and noncompliant groups using a 30-point scale that asked patients how they felt on medication without reference to their levels of knowledge.

The response of health professionals has included the somewhat desperate plea of Vaisrub (1975) in an article entitled "You can lead a horse to water". "No one suggests to the clergy to stop quoting scripture because sin and crime go unabated", wrote the author, who continued, "health education is an ethical imperative". The explanation for the contradictory nature of much of the evidence in this area may lie in the factors that inevitably accompany intensive patient education, factors such as increased contact with interested and motivated health professionals. Cummings, Becker, Kirscht, and Levin (1981) studied the effects of education on the compliance of patients attending for out-patient dialysis. Noting that the improvement in compliance was only temporary, the authors concluded that the change in patient behaviour was the result, not of the information they had received, but of a wish to conform to the authority of the medical staff and to "identify" with their nurse. The behaviour changes described by Blackwell (1976) in patients at risk from cardiovascular disease proved short-lived, although some of the knowledge that they had gained must have persisted. It is possible that the changes were more the result of contact with the educators than consequent on the information itself. The educational steps described by Falloon (1984) are accompanied by a package of measures designed to increase compliance. In the words of Blackwell (1976):

> Even without fear and exhortation, the failure of cognitive learning to change behaviour is hardly surprising in the face of attitudes and reward systems around such fundamental needs as being cared for. A much broader definition of the problem is needed so that education addresses itself not only to knowledge but to motivation and self-management skills.

CHARACTERISTICS OF THE DOCTOR

The effect on compliance of variables related to the personality of the doctor is a subject that has been examined almost exclusively with regard to psychiatric populations. There is ample evidence that different doctors achieve different degrees of compliance, both in a psychotherapeutic setting (Dinnen, 1971) and in a general psychiatry out-patient department (Dodd, 1971). Lowinger and Dobie (1968), examining 456 questionnaires completed by 24 psychiatrists and comparing the responses with the length of time patients stayed in the out-patient clinic, attributed these differences to "attitude factors" in the psychiatrists. Several authors have examined the question of what these attitude factors might be with regard to in- and out-patient attendance and drug compliance.

Examining attendance, Greenwald and Bartemeier (1963) inspected the medical records of 191 patients from a private psychiatric hospital in the United States. They were able to link the frequency of discharges against medical advice with a rating of the "global effectiveness" of the psychiatrist, as assessed by the Clinical Director of the hospital. It is not stated what "global effectiveness" comprised, however, and the conclusion is somewhat circular; presumably one criterion for effectiveness is that the doctor's patients stay in the hospital. Frank, Gliedman, Imber, Nash, and Stone (1957) presented 91 psychiatric out-patients with questionnaires designed to test their attitudes to their doctors, first at their assessment interview and again six months later. The authors identified an "ability to inspire trust" as related to treatment adherence. Katz and Solomon (1958) reviewed the case notes of 353 patients, all those offered treatment by a psychiatric out-patient clinic in the United States in one year. They also rated the attitudes of the therapists as "accepting", "ambivalent", or "nonaccepting" and found that the patients of "accepting" therapists were more likely to remain in treatment. The authors do not explain further the characteristics of such therapists. Gibby, Stotsky, Hiler and Miller (1954) found that psychiatrists rated by patients as "warm", "friendly", and "competent" had less drop-outs from their out-patient clinics. Similar findings were described by Baum, Felzer, D'Zmura, and Shumaker (1966) who found that psychiatrists whose patients remained in treatment were "secure", "aware of patients' needs", "task oriented", and "flexible". The work of Howard et al. (1970) avoided many of the methodological problems affecting the research described earlier, defining terms more clearly and assessing therapists by direct observation rather than by patients' questionnaire responses. The authors observed six experienced psychiatrists during their initial interview with 225 neurotic out-patients. The psychiatrists were rated with regard to their behaviours and personal characteristics, such as how personable and patient they were. Therapists with low drop-out rates were described as more active and more positive in dealing with patients and as conducting a more personalised interview with a clearer structure and focus. The authors concluded that compliance was related more to what therapists did than to what they were like.

Less research exists pertaining to the effect of doctors' attitudes and behaviour on compliance in psychiatric populations in general or in schizophrenics in particular, but therapist characteristics do seem to alter treatment response. Reynolds, Joyce, Swift, Tooley, and Weatherall (1965) undertook a double-blind trial of barbiturates in the treatment of anxiety and noted different responses under different psychiatrists. They concluded that these differences stemmed from the degree to which the therapist emphasised the positive effects of treatment and reassured patients regarding the side-effects of medication. Wheatley (1968) found different rates of improvement on chlordiazepoxide between patients looked after by optimistic, pessimistic, and indifferent doctors. One study that did examine the issue of compliance directly failed to reach statistical significance. Irwin, Weitzel, and Morgan (1971) conducted urine tests to assess the compliance of 40 patients receiving phenothiazines as out-patients. The authors found that 25% of out-patients were nonadherent if they were treated by a doctor who regarded medication as essential in the management of chronic schizophrenia, whereas some 39% were nonadherent if their doctor was ambivalent.

INTERACTION BETWEEN DOCTOR AND PATIENT

Relatively little research has been conducted into the effects of doctor–patient interaction on treatment adherence. This may be because changes in the nature of this interaction have been assumed to be secondary to other variables discussed here, but may also be due to the substantial methodological problems in directly assessing the quality of a medical or psychiatric consultation. Some authors have circumvented this problem by basing their research on patients' and doctors' reports of their interaction, although such reports are likely to be influenced by the respondents' attitudes to illness and treatment.

Research based on these reports has suggested that the quality of the interaction between doctors and patients is important. Korsch and Negrete (1972) observed 800 out-patient consultations in the emergency room of a children's hospital. They reported that mothers who were satisfied with their interview with the doctor were more likely to comply with treatment. Hulka, Cassel, Kupper, and Burdette (1976) studied 357 patients suffering from diabetes or congestive heart failure. In the congestive heart failure group they found that interviews that were rated by patients and doctors as involving good communication of instructions and information were associated with low levels of medication errors.

When the content of interviews has been examined in more detail it appears that simple agreement between doctors and their patients is not associated with improved compliance (Davis, 1968b). One study of the out-patient treatment of chronic schizophrenia goes so far as to suggest that "even extreme disagreements over medication seldom upset an attendance pattern" (Burgoyne, 1976). Most authors have concluded that a successful interview is one where the patient becomes involved in the decision-making process. Thus Schulman (1979) interviewed 99 patients attending two hypertension clinics and asked them to complete a scale measuring "active patient orientation". She reported an association between patients' reports of their compliance and their involvement in treatment. Eisenthal, Emery, Lazare, and Udin (1979) interviewed 130 patients attending the self-referral psychiatric clinic of a general hospital. The authors rated the degree of "negotiation" that had been involved in the interview and found that this was significantly related to subsequent compliance. Hertz, Bernheim, and Perloff (1976) reached similar conclusions in a general practice population. Too powerful a patient role, however, seems to lead to worse compliance. Davis (1968b) tape-recorded 154 new referral interviews in a general medical out-patient clinic and found that the combination of an authoritative patient and an accepting doctor was associated with poor adherence to therapeutic instructions.

The results of this research have not been widely applied in clinical practice. Inui, Yourtee, and Williamson (1976) found that giving tutorials on interview techniques to general physicians improved the compliance of their patients, but these findings have not been replicated in a psychiatric population. It may be that poor doctor–patient interaction may simply reflect other factors associated with poor compliance. In the absence of clear evidence on this point reviewers have limited their advice to recommending that a compliance history be taken in all cases (Morisky, Green, & Levine, 1986) and that in doing so the doctor should concentrate on the positive aspects of the patient's previous treatment adherence (Meichenbaum & Turk, 1987).

ILLNESS VARIABLES

In the field of general medicine, no consistent association has been found between compliance and the seriousness of the patient's condition (as assessed by a doctor) or the number of previous episodes of illness (Meichenbaum & Turk, 1987). Similarly, no association has been found with the proximity of the last episode of ill health or the number or duration of previous admissions to hospital (Baekeland & Lundwall, 1975; Haynes, 1979). Some evidence exists to suggest that a greater degree of disability is associated with improved compliance but, as Haynes (1979) has pointed out, this may well be due to the increased level of supervision that tends to accompany disability. There is general agreement that compliance improves as symptoms become more distressing and declines as symptoms improve or where treatment is entirely prophylactic (Blackwell, 1976; Meichenbaum & Turk, 1987).

In the psychiatric field, some authors have claimed that diagnosis affects compliance. Muller (1962) surveyed 210 instances of absconding from a mental hospital and found that schizophrenics, who represented 41% of the hospital population, comprised 52% of the absconders. Altman, Brown, and Sletten (1972b) found that schizophrenics, along with patients with personality disorders or organic brain syndromes, were more likely to "elope". Carr and Whittenbaugh (1968) contacted 78 psychiatric out-patients by telephone and asked them to participate in a psychotherapy outcome study. Forty-nine patients agreed to participate and 29 did not; the authors found that those who agreed were significantly less likely to be suffering from schizophrenia or borderline schizophrenia. It is not clear, however, to what extent a response to such a request can be extrapolated to measure compliance. Most reviewers have concluded that psychiatric diagnosis has little effect on treatment adherence (Evans & Spelman, 1983; Johnson, 1977). The exception to this rule is mania, where specific factors such as patients "missing" the euphoria of illness and, where symptoms persist, the exaggerated feeling of well-being have been invoked to explain poor compliance (Prien & Caffey, 1977; Schou, Baastrup, Grof, Weis, & Angst, 1970). As with findings in general medical populations, the seriousness with which a doctor regards a patient's complaint does not seem to be associated with the likelihood of that patient refusing treatment. Nor does the number of symptoms present seem to affect compliance. Lipman, Rickels, Uhlenhuth, Park, and Fisher (1965) undertook a six-week, double-blind trial of the use of meprobamate in anxiety neurosis. Compliance was assessed using pill counts and interviews. The authors found, somewhat surprisingly, that the more symptoms a patient presented, the poorer was likely to be the patient's compliance.

In schizophrenia, several elements of patients' psychopathology have been linked to poor compliance. The overall severity of a patient's symptoms may be important but the situation is unclear. Wilson and Enoch (1967) and Bartko et al. (1988) found no association between compliance and general measures of severity, such as disturbed behaviour and thought disorder. Renton et al. (1963) did find an association between the severity of a patient's illness at the time of discharge and the subsequent compliance. The problem in interpreting these studies is that the severity of a patient's symptoms may both result from and cause poor compliance; it becomes impossible to disentangle likely cause and effect. Persecutory delusions were found by Wilson and Enoch (1967) to be commoner in patients who rejected tablets. These conclusions were based on a group of only eight patients who refused chlorpromazine in tablet form but accepted the same drug in a syrup; the implications are unclear. Other authors, working with larger groups of patients, have failed to find any such association (Bartko et al., 1988; Van Putten, Crumpton, & Yale, 1976). The duration of a patient's remission has been invoked by Blackwell (1973) as a possible cause of poor compliance: "The longer a person has remained well, the more he may be prepared to gamble on continued good health." In view of the association between mania and poor compliance, it seems likely that affective features will be related to compliance in schizophrenia. Bartko et al. (1988) studied the drug compliance of 58 schizophrenic subjects all of whom were receiving depot neuroleptic medication. The degree of psychopathology was measured using the Brief Psychiatric Rating Scale (Overall & Gorham, 1962) and compliance was assessed by inspecting the patients' treatment record. It is not clear from the paper at what point the patients' mental state was assessed relative to their defaulting from treatment. The authors found that grandiosity was associated with poor compliance. Van Putten et al. (1976) recorded similar results, using the same measure of psychopathology, when they compared 29 schizophrenics who habitually refused medication with 30 patients who did not.

In general, it is difficult to dispute the conclusion of Haynes (1979), that disease factors are relatively unimportant as determinants of compliance. Schizophrenia and other psychoses are unusual, however, in that the nature of the disease itself may affect a patient's ability to comply. The relationship between insight and compliance was reviewed in the section on psychological characteristics, pp. 9–10. Although the role of the overall level of psychopathology is unclear and one report linking poor adherence to persecutory beliefs has not been replicated, it does seem that grandiosity is associated with reduced compliance.

REFERRAL AND APPOINTMENT SYSTEMS

The distance that patients have to travel does not affect the treatment adherence of the majority (Sackett et al., 1975). The length of time that patients have to wait for appointments has been linked to poor compliance in general medical populations (Rockart & Hofmann, 1969) and in alcoholics (Mayer, 1972; Rosenberg, 1974). In the field of child psychiatry similar findings have been reported by Cohen and Richardson (1970) and by Novick, Benson, and Rembar (1981), both groups undertaking case-control studies of drop-outs from out-patient clinics. Further evidence derives from the work of Gould, Shaffer, and Kaplan (1985) who asked parents the reasons for their child's failure to attend for follow-up. The authors screened 345 children attending an emergency psychiatric service in the United States. Eleven percent of children failed to attend for subsequent appointments and the parents of 11.5% of these gave having to wait a long time for an appointment as the reason for their nonattendance. Related to this may be the fact that 15% said that they had not returned because the child had improved. There is some evidence that if patients do return after a long wait for an appointment, they are then more likely to continue with treatment than those who have been given an appointment straight away (Ross & Lacey, 1961).

The degree of supervision involved in a treatment programme has been shown to be related to compliance. In a general medical population, Sheiner, Rosenberg, Marathe, and Peck (1974) showed a difference of serum digoxin concentrations between out-patients and in-patients. Goldberg, Schooler, Hogarty, and Roper (1977) have emphasised the value of supervision in psychiatric populations where there is general agreement that in-patients are more likely to take their medication than day-patients and that day-patients, in turn, are more likely to do so than out-patients. Hare and Willcox (1967), using urine tests, assessed the compliance with phenothiazine medication of 120 in-patients and 27 day-patients. They found nonadherence rates of 19% and 37%, respectively. Irwin, Weitzel, and Morgan (1971) studied 126 patients receiving phenothiazines, assessing drug compliance by urine analysis. The rates of nonadherence were 7% on a closed ward, 32% on an open ward, 35% in an out-patient clinic, and 63% among patients on hospital leave.

NATURE OF TREATMENT

Aspects of treatment that have been found to be related to compliance include the complexity of the drug regimen, the duration of treatment, the use of depot as opposed to oral phenothiazines, and the presence or absence of side-effects. These will be examined in turn.

In view of the considerable difficulty that many patients experience in understanding drug-taking instructions (Mazzullo, Lasagna, & Grinar, 1974), it might be expected that increasing the complexity of drug regimes would be associated with decreased compliance. The literature broadly supports this view (Davis, 1966). Parkin, Henney, Quirk, and Crooks (1976) followed up 130 patients discharged from an acute medical unit, assessing their compliance using pill counts and interviews. The authors found that when two drugs were prescribed, only 4 out of 48 patients departed from the prescribed dosage, whereas when four drugs were prescribed, 15 out of 35 did so. The only paper to examine this issue with regard to schizophrenia did so only tangentially. Burgoyne (1976) conducted a case-note study to assess the effects of changes in therapeutic regimen on the compliance of 115 patients with chronic schizophrenia. He found that changing the form of treatment had little effect but did not study the relative complexity of the regimens involved. Some debate has surrounded the issue of whether the number of times during the day that medicine has to be taken is a more important variable than the total number of drugs prescribed. Meichenbaum and Turk (1987) have implied that this is the case. Parkin et al. (1976) found that both aspects of complexity were related to compliance, however, and Brand et al. (1977) recorded similar findings in their study of 290 consecutive discharges from a general hospital in Canada.

The relationship between duration of treatment and compliance has been widely studied with regard to general medicine and paediatrics. Bergman and Werner (1963) followed up 59 children who had been prescribed penicillin for upper respiratory tract infections. They found that 56% had stopped taking their tablets after three days and 71% after six. There are numerous difficulties in extrapolating such findings to chronic illnesses where the doctor may intend treatment to continue indefinitely. Haynes (1979) has concluded that the longer the duration of treatment, the higher the chances of the patient dropping out. This would seem to be true almost by definition and it seems likely that it applies in schizophrenia.

The relative value of depot as against oral medication has been investigated specifically with regard to schizophrenia. Johnson and Freeman (1972) followed up 179 patients receiving depot phenothiazines for two years and compared their rate of re-admission to that of the same patients when they were receiving oral medication. The authors found that depot medication reduced the rate of re-admission. That the mediating factor was improved compliance is suggested but not proved by the fact that 40% of patients being re-admitted were not up to date with their medication. Crawford and Forrest (1974) addressed directly the issue of the relationship between route of administration and compliance when they undertook a double-blind trial of fluphenazine decanoate and trifluperazine in the out-patient treatment of schizophrenics. The trial lasted for 40 weeks. Patients receiving their phenothiazines in depot form had a rate of withdrawal from the trial of 14.3%, whereas the equivalent figure for those receiving oral medication was 48.9%. Small numbers (31 patients) prevented this study from reaching statistical significance and no attempt was made to match the groups. On the basis of this and his own work, Freeman (1973) has concluded that the use of depot medication in the management of schizophrenia is associated with improved compliance.

The assumption has usually been made that side-effects of medication are associated with poor compliance and this receives considerable support in the literature pertaining to psychiatry. Michaux (1961) compared the treatment adherence of 142 psychiatric out-patients treated blindly with meprobamate, chlorpromazine, phenobarbitone, and placebo. The author concluded that deviations from prescribed treatment were related to drug side-effects. Similar findings have been reported in drug trials. Porter (1969) undertook a controlled trial of imipramine in the treatment of depression. Of 82 patients in the trial, 19 became overt defaulters and 14 of these were taking drug rather than placebo. A considerable amount of research has focused on schizophrenia. Nelson (1975), using urine analysis, assessed the compliance of 120 newly admitted male schizophrenics and found that it was reduced where drug side-effects were present; Falloon, Watt, and Shepherd (1978) have reported similar results. Other evidence comes from the mouths of patients. Renton et al. (1963) undertook a 12-month follow-up of 132 schizophrenic patients discharged from in-patient care in Edinburgh. The authors found that 46% of patients failed to take their medication as instructed. The reasons given by patients were, first, that they now "felt alright" and no longer required medication and, second, that they experienced side-effects from their treatment. Van Putten (1974) has suggested that akathisia is more closely related to poor compliance than are other side-effects of phenothiazines.

The evidence in this area is, however, far from unequivocal. Parkes et al. (1962) studied 96 schizophrenic patients discharged to general practitioner follow-up. Fifty-five patients failed to take treatment as their doctors intended but only seven of these blamed drug side-effects. Haynes (1979) reviewed 13 studies from all fields of medicine where patients were asked the reasons for their poor compliance. He found that side-effects were blamed in only 5–10% of cases. Further doubt is cast on the clarity of the link between drug side-effects and poor compliance by the work of Willcox, Gillan, and Hare (1965) who examined the drug compliance of psychiatric out-patients receiving either chlorpromazine or imipramine. Compliance was assessed using urine analysis and side-effects by direct observation in a routine out-patient clinic. The authors found that, among patients receiving chlorpromazine, those who experienced drug side-effects defaulted less (45%) than those who did not (56%). An explanation for this result has been put forward by Irwin et al. (1971) who assessed the compliance of 40 patients receiving phenothiazines in an out-patient setting. The authors argued that good compliance could result from the presence of side-effects because the patient would then be sure that the drug was "doing something". In conclusion, it would seem inevitable that side-effects, when severe, will be associated with poor compliance. When they are less troublesome, however, their effect on treatment adherence is equivocal. When they are present in schizophrenia, there is some evidence that akathisia is more closely associated with poor compliance than are other extra-pyramidal symptoms.

CHAPTER TWO

Aims of the research

The literature review identified a number of factors associated with compliance. The present research was designed to test these associations using a prospective study design in a group of patients with schizophrenia. In addition to the variables already described, two factors that have not been widely investigated, namely, compulsory detention and previous compliance, were examined. In general terms, therefore, the aim of the study was to identify those factors that are associated with compliance in schizophrenia. In particular, a number of predictions were being tested. These are:

1. Patients of low socioeconomic status and low social stability will comply poorly with treatment.
2. Patients with insight will show better compliance than other patients.
3. Patients treated with complex drug regimens, oral medication, and suffering from the side-effects of medication will comply poorly.
4. Patients who have been compulsorily detained during their admission will comply poorly.
5. Patients with a history of previous poor compliance will again comply poorly.

CHAPTER THREE

Method

PROCEDURE

The study was a prospective investigation of the factors associated with compliance in 61 patients with a ward diagnosis of schizophrenia discharged from the Bethlem and Maudsley Hospital between May and December 1988. Subjects were identified through regular liaison with ward staff. In addition to having a ward diagnosis of schizophrenia, entry criteria for the study required that a patient had been an in-patient for at least two weeks and that the patient's discharge was planned within two weeks. Seventy-four patients were identified as fulfilling the entry criteria. Of these, 11 were unavailable for interview, usually because they were receiving extended periods of hospital leave. The remaining 63 patients were approached for consent. Two of these refused, leaving a study population of 61. All subjects who gave consent were interviewed and their medical records examined. These procedures allowed information to be collected regarding sociodemographic details, the subject's insight and attitudes, treatment details, illness details, and previous compliance with treatment. Sixty-one subjects (100% of sample) were traced to assess their compliance with out-patient attendance and drug treatment at one and two years. This allowed information to be collected regarding compliance with drug treatment and out-patient attendance. Where follow-up care took place in the hospital out-patient department, these details were obtained by inspection of medical records and prescription cards, and by urinary drug testing of patients receiving only oral medication. Where follow-up took place in a general practice setting, compliance with out-patient attendance was assessed by interviewing the health worker who saw the patient the most, usually the general practitioner or a community psychiatric nurse. Compliance with drug treatment, where the subject received depot medication, was assessed at this interview and, where the subject received only oral medication, by urinary drug testing.

VARIABLES

Sociodemographic

The patient's age, sex, employment status, and ethnic origin were recorded along with where the patient would be living after discharge. Information was collected regarding where the patient received the majority of follow-up care. Where a patient received care from more than one source (e.g. GP and community psychiatric nurse), care was regarded as being provided by the person with whom the patient spent most time. In the results section "DSC" refers to follow-up in the District Services Centre, the community psychiatric services at the Maudsley Hospital.

Patient insight and attitude

The subjects were asked six questions designed to assess their level of insight and their attitude to their illness. These questions were:

> "Do you think you have been unwell during this admission?"
> "Do you think you will become ill again?"
> "Did treatment help?"
> "Will you take treatment after your discharge?"
> "Will you ever get back to your old self?"
> "Why were you in hospital?"

The answers to the first five questions were recorded as "yes" or "no". The answer to the sixth question was interpreted by the interviewer and recorded as showing insight (e.g. "Because I got ill") or a lack of insight (e.g. "Because my family don't like me").

Subjects were also presented with an attitude assessment instrument based on the work of Soskis and Bowers (1969). The instrument consists of a list of statements grouped under six headings: "insight positive", "insight negative", "illness positive", "illness negative", "future positive", and "future negative"; the full list of statements appears in the Appendix. Five statements appear under each heading. The patient was presented with a list (in random order) of all the statements shown and asked to state which applied to him or her. The number of statements under each heading that, in the patient's opinion, applied to them was recorded.

Illness details
Information from the records of the admission was used to rate the presence or absence of delusions, hallucinations, mood change, and thought disorder. Cognitive function was assessed using the Mini Mental State Examination (Folstein, Folstein, & McHugh, 1975). Other information collected for descriptive purposes included, for first admissions, the length of time unwell before admission and the duration of admission and, for subsequent admissions, the age of onset of the illness, the number of discrete episodes of illness, and the length of time unwell on this occasion before admission.

Treatment details
Details of the therapeutic regimen on which the patient was to be discharged were recorded at time of discharge and this information was checked at the time of follow-up. It was recorded how often a patient received medication, how many drugs he or she received and whether the medication was received in depot or oral form. Information regarding drug side-effects was obtained at interview prior to discharge. Patients were asked to say whether or not they suffered from each side-effect in turn. Akathisia was described to the patient as "a feeling of restlessness such that you can't keep still", akinesia as "slowness in your movements", drowsiness as "tiredness", tremor as "tremor or shakiness", and dystonia as "stiffness in your muscles".

Compulsory detention
It was recorded whether or not the patient had been compulsorily detained during the index admission.

Previous compliance
Information from the medical records was used to assess whether the patient had previously defaulted from out-patient attendance or drug treatment.

Outcome

Outcome was measured in terms of compliance with out-patient attendance and with drug treatment at one and two years. In the case of out-patient compliance, this was rated as "good", "average", or "poor" according to whether the patient attended more than 75%, between 25 and 75%, or less than 25% of the out-patient appointments. Ratings were derived from examination of case-notes at follow-up.

In the case of compliance with drug treatment, this was rated as "good", "average", or "poor" according to whether the patient had received more than 75%, between 25 and 75%, or less than 25% of the prescribed medication. Of the cohort of 61 patients, 59 were alive at two years. Of these, 33 were receiving drug treatment at two years (all of those with "good" drug compliance plus three of those with "average" drug compliance). Of these 33, 22 patients were receiving depot neuroleptics. Where treatment was received in the hospital out-patient department, the prescription record was consulted to establish the extent of compliance; where a patient was receiving treatment in the community, the general practioner or community psychiatric nurse responsible was consulted.

Eleven patients were receiving neuroleptics in oral form only; compliance in these cases was assessed by urinary drug testing. All patients who were asked to provide a urine sample did so. The test consisted of alkaline extraction into chloroform followed by thin-layer chromatography, and yielded a positive or a negative result. It was not possible to measure quantitatively the presence of drugs or breakdown products in the samples. In four cases urine tests conducted as part of the study proved positive for neuroleptics. In a further four cases it was not possible to test for the particular neuroleptic prescribed but urinary testing confirmed compliance with other psychotropic medication prescribed simultaneously. In three cases it was not possible to test for the particular neuroleptic being taken or for other psychotropic medication. The doctors responsible for the care of these patients were questioned in detail. All patients were attending regularly and without prompting to collect their prescriptions. One provided a urine sample in the knowledge that it was to be used to assess compliance (before the author realised that no test was available). All were therefore included in the "good" compliance group.

STATISTICAL ANALYSIS

Statistical associations were examined using the chi-square test. The reliability of this test is reduced where cell numbers are small. For this reason, where an association was found to be statistically significant to the $P < 0.05$ level using the chi-square, this significance was re-examined using an Exact test. In all cases that were re-examined the statistical significance was maintained.

CHAPTER FOUR

Results

SAMPLE

The sample consisted of 33 men (54%) and 28 women (46%). The mean age was 35.9 years (SD 12.76, range 18–68). Forty (65.6%) were white, 17 (27.9%) black, and 4 (6.5%) of Asian descent or of mixed race. Of those who were black, 2 were born in the United Kingdom and 15 overseas, usually in the West Indies. All patients were re-diagnosed using R.D.C. criteria (Spitzer et al., 1978). Twenty-eight fulfilled the criteria for definite schizophrenia and 19 the criteria for probable schizophrenia. Of the 14 who fulfilled the criteria for neither, 10 had fulfilled the diagnostic criteria for definite or probable schizophrenia during a previous admission. The remaining four patients never fulfilled the criteria for schizophrenia. Two were subsequently diagnosed as suffering from affective illnesses and two from personality disorder.

For 12 patients, this was their first admission to hospital. The mean age of these patients was 28.7 years (SD 11.08, range 18–51). They had been unwell for an average of 58.7 weeks prior to admission (SD 39.8, range 1–98) and their mean time in hospital was 10.67 weeks (SD 6.75, range 1–20). Forty-nine patients had been in hospital before. The mean age of these patients was 37.27 years (SD 12.68, range 19–68). The mean age of onset of their illness was 26.67 years (SD 9.61, range 13–59) and they had experienced a mean of 6.48 discrete episodes (SD 4.04, range 2–20). The mean duration of relapse prior to admission was 9.80 weeks (SD 19.51, range 1–98).

Of 61 patients, all were alive at one year follow-up and two had committed suicide by the time of two year follow-up. At one year, the compliance with out-patient attendance of 14 (22.9%) was "poor", that of 9 (14.7%) was "average", and that of 38 (62.4%) was "good" (for definition of "poor", "average", and "good" see Chapter 3, p.30) and the corresponding figures for compliance with drug treatment at one year were 15 (24.6%), 10 (16.4%), and 36 (59.0%). At two years, the compliance with out-patient attendance of 18 (30.5%) was "poor", that of 7 (11.9%) was "average", and that of 34 (57.6%) was "good". The corresponding figures for compliance with drug treatment at two years were 19 (32.2%), 10 (16.9%), and 30 (50.9%).

SOCIODEMOGRAPHIC FACTORS

Sociodemographic data were available for 60 of the 61 subjects. Age, sex, ethnicity, and employment status were not found significantly to be associated with out-patient or treatment compliance.

The relationship between destination on discharge and subsequent compliance is shown in Tables 4.1 and 4.2.

Patients who were discharged to their families or friends were more likely to comply with clinic attendance than those who lived alone or in hostels, although the level of significance was low. When destination on discharge was examined with regard to compliance with medication at one and two years similar trends were found.

The setting in which patients received treatment was studied with regard to subsequent out-patient compliance and the results are shown in Tables 4.3 and 4.4.

TABLE 4.1
Relationship between destination on discharge and compliance with out-patient attendance at one year

Compliance	Family (%)	Hostel (%)	Alone (%)	Friends (%)
poor	5 (2)	4 (57)	5 (20)	0 (0)
average	2 (8)	1 (14)	6 (24)	0 (0)
good	18 (72)	2 (29)	14 (56)	3 (100)

Chi-square = 9.51 with 6 df.; $P = 0.15$.

TABLE 4.2
Relationship between destination on discharge and
compliance with out-patient attendance at two years

Compliance	Family (%)	Hostel (%)	Alone (%)	Friends (%)
poor	7 (28)	4 (67)	7 (29)	0 (0)
average	1 (4)	0 (0)	6 (25)	0 (0)
good	17 (68)	2 (33)	11 (46)	3 (100)

Chi-square = 11.87 with 6 df, $P = 0.06$.

TABLE 4.3
Relationship between treatment setting and
compliance with out-patient attendance at one year

Compliance	OPD (%)	DSC (%)	Day Pt (%)	GP (%)	CPN (%)
poor	12 (26)	0 (0)	2 (33)	0 (0)	0 (0)
average	6 (13)	0 (0)	0 (0)	1 (33)	2 (67)
good	28 (61)	2 (100)	4 (67)	2 (67)	1 (33)

Chi-square = 10.51 with 8 df, $P = 0.23$.

TABLE 4.4
Relationship between treatment setting and
compliance with out-patient attendance at two years

Compliance	OPD (%)	DSC (%)	Day Pt (%)	GP (%)	CPN (%)
poor	16 (36)	0 (0)	2 (40)	0 (0)	0 (0)
average	4 (9)	0 (0)	0 (0)	1 (33)	2 (67)
good	25 (56)	2 (100)	3 (60)	2 (67)	1 (33)

Chi-square = 13.68 with 8 df, $P = 0.09$.

The figures show that the large majority of patients were followed up in an out-patient setting. The differences in compliance between these patients and those who were followed up elsewhere were not significant. When treatment setting was examined with regard to treatment compliance at one and two years the results were similar and no significant differences were found between the groups.

PATIENT INSIGHT AND ATTITUDE

A patient's insight was tested by asking several questions at interview; data were available for all subjects. In response to the question "Do you think you have been unwell during this admission?", there was no significant difference between compliers and noncompliers with respect to out-patient attendance at one or two years or treatment at one year. Only with respect to compliance with treatment at two years was there any difference and here the statistical significance was low (see Table 4.5). When patients were asked "Do you think you will become ill again?", there was no significant difference between the answers of those who subsequently complied and those who did not. The subsequent compliance of patients who responded to the question "Did treatment help?" is shown in Tables 4.6, 4.7, 4.8, and 4.9.

The answer to the question "Did treatment help?" was more likely to be yes in patients with good compliance. A positive response to the question "Will you take treatment after discharge?" was associated with good drug compliance at one year and good out-patient compliance at two years, as shown in Tables 4.10 and 4.11. There was also an association between a positive answer to this question and both out-patient compliance at one year and drug compliance at two years, although with lower levels of significance ($P < 0.06$). No statistically significant associations with compliance were found in the responses to the question "Will you ever get back to your old self?" or in the

TABLE 4.5
Relationship between the answer to the question "Do you think you have been unwell during this admission?" and compliance with drug treatment at two years

Compliance	No (%)	Yes (%)
poor	6 (55)	13 (27)
average	3 (27)	7 (15)
good	2 (18)	28 (58)

Chi-square = 5.78 with 2 *df*, $P = 0.06$.

TABLE 4.6
Relationship between the answer to the question "Did treatment help?"
and compliance with out-patient attendance at one year

Compliance	No (%)	Yes (%)
poor	6 (50)	8 (16)
average	1 (8)	8 (16)
good	5 (42)	33 (67)

Chi-square = 6.20 with 2 df; P = 0.05.

TABLE 4.7
Relationship between the answer to the question "Did treatment help?"
and compliance with drug treatment at one year

Compliance	No (%)	Yes (%)
poor	8 (67)	7 (14)
average	1 (8)	9 (18)
good	3 (25)	33 (67)

Chi-square = 14.28 with 2 df; P = < 0.001.

TABLE 4.8
Relationship between the answer to the question "Did treatment help?"
and compliance with out-patient attendance at two years

Compliance	No (%)	Yes (%)
poor	8 (67)	10 (21)
average	1 (8)	3 (13)
good	3 (25)	31 (66)

Chi-square = 9.37 with 2 df; P = < 0.01.

TABLE 4.9
Relationship between the answer to the question "Did treatment help?"
and compliance with drug treatment at two years

Compliance	No (%)	Yes (%)
poor	9 (75)	10 (21)
average	1 (8)	9 (19)
good	2 (17)	28 (60)

Chi-square = 12.69 with 2 df, P = < 0.002.

TABLE 4.10
Relationship between the answer to the question "Will you take treatment after
discharge?" and compliance with drug treatment at one year

Compliance	No (%)	Yes (%)
poor	5 (71)	10 (19)
average	1 (14)	9 (17)
good	1 (14)	35 (65)

Chi-square = 9.76 with 2 df, P = < 0.01.

TABLE 4.11
Relationship between the answer to the question "Will you take treatment after
discharge?" and compliance with out-patient attendance at two years

Compliance	No (%)	Yes (%)
poor	5 (71)	13 (25)
average	0 (0)	7 (13)
good	2 (29)	32 (62)

Chi-square = 6.46 with 2 df, P = < 0.04.

interviewer-rated insight revealed in the answer to the question "Why do you think you were in hospital?"

With regard to patient attitudes, data were available for 56 subjects. "Insight positive", "insight negative", "illness positive", "illness negative", and "future negative" views were not found to be associated with compliance. "Future positive" views were found to be associated with good out-patient compliance one year after discharge, as shown in Table 4.12. In addition, when the figures for "poor" and "average" compliance were combined to allow comparison between good compliers and all other patients, a "future positive" attitude was associated with good out-patient and treatment compliance at one year (see Tables 4.13 and 4.14).

These associations did not persist to two-year follow-up when the P values for the link between a "future positive" attitude and, first, out-patient compliance and, second, drug treatment were 0.08 and 0.18, respectively.

ILLNESS VARIABLES

The presence or absence of thought disorder, delusions, hallucinations, and mood change at index presentation was examined and no significant association was found between any of these variables and subsequent compliance. In the case of delusions, a nonsignificant trend towards the association of abnormal beliefs with poor compliance was found, as shown in Table 4.15. Data were available for 60 of the 61 subjects.

Assessment of cognitive function was discontinued after 38 subjects had been interviewed; 36 of these were alive at two years. No association was found between cognitive function and out-patient attendance at two years; the results are shown in Table 4.16.

There was a similar lack of association between cognitive function and the other outcome measures, namely, compliance with out-patient attendance at one year and compliance with drug treatment at one and two years.

TREATMENT VARIABLES

The associations between the number of drugs being taken on discharge from hospital and compliance with treatment one year after discharge are shown in Table 4.17. Data were available for all 61 subjects.

There is no significant association between the number of drugs being taken on discharge and drug compliance one year later. Similar analyses

TABLE 4.12
Relationship between number of "future positive" statements and compliance with out-patient attendance at one year

Compliance	0, 1, 2 (%)	3, 4, 5 (%)
poor	5 (65)	8 (22)
average	6 (32)	3 (8)
good	8 (42)	26 (70)

Chi-square = 6.06 with 2 df, $P = < 0.05$.

TABLE 4.13
Relationship between number of "future positive" statements and compliance with out-patient attendance at one year

Compliance	0, 1, 2 (%)	3, 4, 5 (%)
good	8 (42)	26 (70)
all other	11 (58)	11 (30)

Chi-square = 4.17 with 1 df, $P = < 0.05$.

TABLE 4.14
Relationship between number of "future positive" statements and compliance with drug treatment at one year

Compliance	0, 1, 2 (%)	3, 4, 5 (%)
good	7 (37)	25 (68)
all others	12 (63)	12 (32)

Chi-square = 4.48 with 1 df, $P = < 0.03$.

TABLE 4.15
**Relationship between the presence of delusions at index admission
and compliance with out-patient attendance at one year**

Compliance	No delusions (%)	Delusions (%)
poor	3 (20)	10 (22)
average	0 (0)	9 (20)
good	12 (80)	26 (58)

Chi-square = 3.90 with 2 *df*, *P* = 0.14.

TABLE 4.16
**Relationship between Mini Mental State score
and compliance with out-patient attendance at one year**

Compliance	< 27 (%)	27, 28 (%)	29, 30 (%)
poor	4 (50)	3 (43)	7 (33)
average	0 (0)	0 (0)	3 (14)
good	4 (50)	4 (57)	11 (52)

Chi-square = 1.65 with 4 *df*, *P* = 0.82.

TABLE 4.17
**Relationship between number of drugs being taken at discharge
and compliance with drug treatment at one year**

Compliance	1, 2 drugs (%)	3, 4 drugs (%)	> 4 drugs (%)
poor	10 (26)	4 (21)	1 (25)
average	6 (16)	3 (16)	1 (25)
good	22 (58)	12 (63)	2 (50)

Chi-square = 0.45 with 4 *df*, *P* = 0.98.

were conducted comparing the number of drugs prescribed with compliance with out-patient attendance at one and two years and with compliance with drug treatment at two years; here again, no significant association was found.

The number of times during the day at which medication was prescribed was recorded and compared with drug compliance one year after discharge. Data were available for 60 of the 61 subjects and the results are shown in Table 4.18. Where a patient received depot medication only, daily medication frequency was recorded as "0".

The number of times per day at which a patient was prescribed to take medication was also compared with out-patient compliance at one and two years and with compliance with drug treatment at two years; no significant associations were found.

TABLE 4.18
Relationship between number of times per day patient is required to take medication and compliance with drug treatment at one year

Compliance	0 (%)	1/d (%)	2/d (%)	3/d (%)	4/d (%)
poor	2 (40)	1 (8)	3 (20)	6 (37)	2 (17)
average	1 (20)	4 (33)	0 (0)	3 (19)	2 (17)
good	2 (40)	7 (58)	12 (80)	7 (44)	8 (67)

Chi-square = 10.14 with 8 df, $P = 0.26$.

TABLE 4.19
Relationship between mode of administration of medication and compliance with drug treatment at one year

Compliance	Depot (%)	Oral only (%)
poor	10 (29)	5 (19)
average	5 (15)	5 (19)
good	19 (56)	17 (63)

Chi-square = 0.99 with 2 df, $P = 0.61$.

The drug compliance at one year of patients who received depot medication was compared with that of those who received oral medication only and the results are shown in Table 4.19; data were available for all subjects.

The mode of treatment administration was also compared with out-patient compliance at one and two years and with compliance with drug treatment at two years; no significant associations were found.

When the effect of drug side-effects was studied, data were available for all 59 subjects who were alive at two years. Akathisia, drowsiness, tremor, and dystonia were not found to be associated significantly with compliance. Only with akinesia was an association found (see Table 4.20).

A similar trend was noted with respect to compliance with drug treatment at one year.

Forty-six of the subjects who were alive at two years had received neuroleptic medication prior to the index admission. When the effect of a patient's ever having experienced side-effects of medication in the past was studied, akathisia, akinesia, drowsiness, and dystonia were not significantly associated with compliance. The association between previous tremor and compliance is shown in Table 4.21.

COMPULSORY DETENTION

Patients who had been detained under the Mental Health Act were compared with those who had not been so detained and the effects on compliance noted. The results are shown in Tables 4.22 and 4.23. There is a statistically significant correlation between compulsory detention

TABLE 4.20
Relationship between akinesia
and compliance with drug treatment at two years

Compliance	No akinesia (%)	Akinesia (%)
poor	10 (31)	9 (33)
average	2 (6)	8 (30)
good	20 (63)	10 (37)

Chi-square = 6.61 with 2 *df*; $P = < 0.04$.

TABLE 4.21
Relationship between previous experience of tremor
and compliance with drug treatment at two years

Compliance	No previous tremor (%)	Previous tremor (%)
poor	9 (28)	5 (36)
average	1 (3)	7 (50)
good	22 (69)	2 (14)

Chi-square = 18.03 with 2 *df*, *P* = < 0.001.

TABLE 4.22
Relationship between compulsory detention
and compliance with out-patient attendance at one year

Compliance	Not detained (%)	Detained (%)
poor	5 (12)	8 (42)
average	8 (20)	1 (5)
good	28 (68)	10 (53)

Chi-square = 7.62 with 2 *df*, *P* = < 0.03.

TABLE 4.23
Relationship between compulsory detention
and compliance with out-patient attendance at two years

Compliance	Not detained (%)	Detained (%)
poor	8 (21)	10 (53)
average	9 (23)	1 (5)
good	22 (56)	8 (42)

Chi-square = 7.10 with 2 *df*, *P* = < 0.03.

and both out-patient compliance at one year and treatment compliance at two years. Analysis of the correlations of compulsory detention with out-patient compliance at two years and treatment compliance at one year showed similar trends.

PREVIOUS COMPLIANCE

Fifty-seven subjects had received drug treatment for psychiatric complaints prior to the index admission. Previous failure to adhere to treatment regimens was significantly associated with failed drug compliance at one year, as shown in Table 4.24. This significant association was maintained when the relationship between previous poor adherence to treatment and compliance with out-patient attendance was examined ($P < 0.01$ at one year and $P < 0.05$ at two years) and was similarly maintained when comparison was made with compliance with drug treatment at two years ($P < 0.05$).

The relationship between previous failure to attend out-patients and failure to attend one year after discharge is shown in Table 4.25.

Previous failed out-patient attendance was also found to be associated with poor drug treatment adherence at one and two years ($P < 0.0001$ and $P < 0.005$, respectively) and poor compliance with out-patient treatment at two years ($P < 0.005$).

TABLE 4.24
Relationship between previous failed treatment adherence
and failed drug compliance at one year

Compliance	Previous adherer (%)	Previous failure (%)
poor	3 (11)	10 (34)
average	0 (0)	10 (34)
good	25 (89)	9 (31)

Chi-square = 21.29 with 2 df.; P = < 0.001.

TABLE 4.25
Relationship between previous failed out-patient attendance
and compliance with out-patient attendance at one year

Compliance	Previous adherer (%)	Previous failure (%)
poor	2 (7)	11 (38)
average	1 (4)	7 (24)
good	25 (89)	11 (38)

Chi-square = 16.16 with 2 *df.*; *P* = < 0.001.

FURTHER STATISTICAL ANALYSIS

In an attempt to establish to what extent the various variables discussed act independently to affect compliance, the previously noted association between compulsory detention and drug compliance at two years was retested, controlling for previous compliance with treatment. The results are shown in Table 4.26. Data were available for 54 of the 55 subjects, alive at two years, who had received treatment for a psychiatric condition prior to the index admission.

It is clear that the effect of compulsory detention does not disappear when previous compliance is controlled for, but the numbers are small. Similar problems with sample size were encountered when attempts were made to investigate the degree of interaction of other variables using the same technique. Three-way tables analysed through a log-linear model in GLIM (Royal Statistical Society, 1986) proved unreliable owing to the sample size.

TABLE 4.26
**Relationship between compulsory detention and drug compliance at two years,
controlling for previous drug compliance**

Previous good compliance

Compliance	Not detained (%)	Detained (%)
poor	2 (12)	1 (14)
average	3 (19)	0 (0)
good	11 (69)	6 (86)

Chi-square = 1.514 with 2 *df.*; $P = 0.47$.

Previous failed compliance

Compliance	Not detained (%)	Detained (%)
poor	5 (25)	8 (73)
average	6 (30)	1 (9)
good	9 (45)	2 (18)

Chi-square = 6.67 with 2 *df.*; $P = < 0.05$.

CHAPTER FIVE

The findings in the light of previous work

SOCIODEMOGRAPHIC FACTORS

The literature review concluded that low socioeconomic status and social stability are associated with poor compliance in psychiatric populations. This was tested by comparing patients' employment status and destination on discharge with their subsequent compliance. Employment status was not found to be associated with compliance. It should be noted, however, that only 11 of the sample were employed at the time of admission and that, of these, eight showed good compliance with drug treatment at one year. Of those who were unemployed at the time of admission, only 28 out of 59 showed good compliance. The failure to reach statistical significance may be a product of the small sample. With regard to destination on discharge, the trend towards improved compliance in patients living with their families is consistent with the findings of other workers that greater social stability is associated with improved adherence to psychiatric treatment.

PATIENT INSIGHT AND ATTITUDE

The literature review suggested that patients with insight were more likely to comply with treatment than others. It also suggested that positive attitudes to illness in general, their own illness, treatment in general, and their own treatment were likely to be associated with improved compliance.

The results suggest that the relationship between insight, attitudes, and compliance is complicated. The first test of insight, asking the patient "Do you think you have been unwell during this admission?", was associated with subsequent compliance only at two years and then with only a low level of significance. The response to a further question, "Why were you in hospital?", was rated by the interviewer as showing a presence or absence of insight. Insight rated in this way was not associated with compliance. Finally, the "insight positive" measure developed by Soskis and Bowers (1969) collates positive responses to such statements as "The thing that really counts is understanding why you feel the way you do" and "Now that I understand why I became ill I can handle my problems better". No association was found between a high score on this measure and subsequent compliance. One explanation for these findings, which appear to contradict those of other authors, is that the measures used did not constitute true measures of insight. This is probably the case with regard to the measure designed by Soskis and Bowers, where the attitude being measured seems to concern the patient's feelings in general rather than those pertaining to illness and treatment in particular. It probably does not explain why the responses to the questions "Do you think you have been unwell during this admission?" and "Why were you in hospital?" were not associated with compliance. These questions are close to the core of modern concept of insight in psychosis.

The response to the question "Did treatment help?" was associated with subsequent compliance with medication with a high level of statistical significance; of all the questions asked regarding insight and attitude, the response to this most strongly predicted adherence. The response to the question "Will you take treatment after your discharge?" was also significantly associated with compliance. These questions, concentrating on specific opinions regarding a particular course of treatment, proved to be more powerful predictors of compliance than more general, even philosophical, enquiries about whether patients regarded themselves as ill.

The composite measures of attitude developed by Soskis and Bowers (1969), "insight positive", "insight negative", "future negative", "illness positive", and "illness negative", were not associated with compliance. The only composite measure that did show such an association was "future positive". This measure collates positive answers to statements such as "If I have to go to hospital again I think I will recover" and "Whatever happens in the future I think I will be able to handle it". It thus represents a measure of what could otherwise be termed "optimism". It may be of note that although this was associated with out-patient compliance at one year, this effect was lost by the time of two-year follow-up. The significant negative finding in this area is that a positive attitude to one's own illness was not associated with improved compliance. This is in contradiction to the findings of other authors. The explanation may lie in the particular statements chosen by Soskis and Bowers to make up "illness positive". Statements such as "It was a turning point in my life—since then things have got better" may reflect more a lack of realism than a positive attitude.

The conclusions of other authors, that insight is associated with improved compliance, have generally not been confirmed. More strongly associated with compliance were a positive attitude to the patient's own treatment ("Did treatment help?", "Will you take treatment after your discharge?") and an optimistic view of the future.

ILLNESS VARIABLES

The literature review suggested that delusions and affective change may be associated with decreased compliance. This was not confirmed by this work. The explanation for the discrepancy probably lies in the numbers involved in the various studies. The association between persecutory delusions and poor compliance is a fragile one, based on one study with small numbers and not supported by subsequent research. The reported association with affective change refers to hypomanic symptoms. Although mood change was noted in 20 of the patients in this study, the symptoms were those of depression in all but two cases.

TREATMENT VARIABLES

The literature review suggested that the use of a simple treatment regimen, the use of depot medication, and the absence of side-effects of medication, especially akathisia, were all associated with improved compliance. In this study the complexity of the treatment regime and the use of depot medication were not associated with improved compliance. Side-effects at the time of discharge from hospital bore little relationship to subsequent compliance and where there was a relationship,this was with akinesia.

The lack of an association between the complexity of the treatment regime and compliance may reflect the generally low complexity of the regimes used. Thirty-eight patients were receiving two drugs or fewer and in 33 of these one was a depot injection. Only four patients were receiving four drugs or more. A similar argument cannot be employed, however, with regard to the frequency with which patients were supposed to take medication during the day. Twenty-eight subjects were prescribed medication three or four times per day at discharge without any associated decline in their compliance. One explanation might be that the complexity of the regime had already been accurately titrated against the patient's capacity to understand and comply. It seems reasonable to assume that the complexity of the treatment regime will only impinge on compliance in as far as it is seen as a problem by the patient. Where this has already been taken into account, and the regime altered accordingly, the link between complexity and compliance could be expected to disappear. With the exception of one report by Van Putten (1974), the association between akinesia and poor compliance has not been widely noted. The pattern of the association, a trend at one year and statistically significant at two years, and the specificity of this link to compliance with drug treatment and not to compliance with out-patient attendance, suggests that it is genuine. It may be that akinesia as a side-effect is particularly unsettling for patients. It may also be that the physical aspects of compliance, such as finding medication or getting to a depot clinic, are rendered more problematic. The association between a previous experience of tremor and poor compliance seems to contradict the finding that tremor at the time of interview was not associated with compliance. It may be that previous tremor predicts future tremor and that patients who had experienced this side-effect before went on to do so again, after the research interview. It is still not clear why tremor should then be associated with stopping medication when tremor at the time of interview is not. In addition, the pattern of results shown in Table 4.21 demonstrates no continuum from good, through average to poor compliance. It may be that the association between a previous experience of tremor and poor compliance is a chance finding.

COMPULSORY DETENTION

Patients who had been compulsorily detained were significantly less likely than other patients to comply with treatment at two years and with out-patient attendance at one year. Similar trends, with less statistical significance, were noted for the other outcome measures. It may be that the experience of being detained at index admission renders a subject hostile to future attempts to engage him in care. It may also be that a patient's requirement for compulsory detention simply reflects poor compliance in the past. An attempt was made to disentangle these factors by controlling for previous compliance and by log-linear analysis. It appeared that the two variables, compulsory detention and previous failed compliance, affect compliance independently, but the numbers involved were too small to draw firm conclusions.

PREVIOUS COMPLIANCE

One of the most commonly reported findings in compliance research is that past behaviour predicts future behaviour. This is confirmed by the study findings.

CHAPTER SIX

Implications for clinical practice and future research

What are the implications of this research for the way in which individual patients are managed and the direction future investigations of compliance in schizophrenia should take? Before any such implications can be discussed some caveats must be inserted. First, the degree to which conclusions can be drawn from a sample of this size will always be limited. In particular, it has not been possible to control for variables that are already known to affect compliance when investigating new associations. Second, the study is quantitative in nature. No attempt has been made to obtain an understanding of the way in which patients make their decisions as to whether or not to attend for out-patient follow-up or take medication. The complementary approach to the one adopted here, one that might offer valuable information as to the likely benefits of various interventions aimed at improving compliance, would be a qualitative, interview-based study examining individual attitudes to illness in more detail and investigating the relative weight that patients themselves attach to drug side-effects, reduced psychotic symptomatology, and the like.

Third, a number of the factors, identified in the literature review as likely contributors to compliance, could not be investigated in a study of this type. The attitudes and approaches of health workers in general and of doctors prescribing medication in particular have been shown to be important contributors to whether or not patients take their treatment as prescribed. Doctors who adopt a structured approach to the issue of medication and who appear themselves to have confidence in the drugs that they are using seem to encourage compliance in their patients. The related subject of the nature of the interaction between the doctor and the patient and the design of referral and appointment systems have also been shown to have important roles to play, roles that have not been investigated here. With these reservations this study is one of the few prospective investigations of compliance in schizophrenia and some guarded suggestions are in order.

With regard to socioeconomic factors, however, suggestions relating to clinical practice are likely to be few. Not only were these factors shown here to be relatively unimportant contributors to compliance, but they are also relatively immune to clinical intervention. The value of further research into the effect of variables such as age, sex, and socioeconomic status must similarly be regarded as questionable. Earlier research on larger patient populations has shown age and income effects, however, and it would be wrong to exclude socioeconomic factors from future analyses. There should be a continuing requirement in compliance research to ensure that groups are matched in terms of socioeconomics before their compliance is compared.

With regard to insight and the patient's attitude to his or her illness, the findings reported here and those of other authors are likely to be of more interest. First, loss of insight is a common symptom of schizophrenia, described in 97% of the World Health Organisation sample of acute cases (World Health Organisation, 1973). Second, it provides one of the few examples of a psychiatric symptom that appears to impinge directly on compliance. This is the case in both in-patient (Bartko et al., 1988; Lin et al., 1979; Marder et al., 1983; McEvoy et al., 1989; Nelson, 1975) and out-patient (Heinrichs et al., 1985) populations. The intriguing possibility arises that better treatment might result in better compliance.

Insight is likely to be important then, but several issues remain to be elucidated. For one thing, the nature of the link between lack of insight and schizophrenia is unclear. It is tempting to draw comparisons with the responses to their symptoms of patients with tardive dyskinesia. Usually regarded as a side-effect of treatment with phenothiazines, tardive dyskinesia is a frequent concomitant of schizophrenia. Many sufferers are remarkably unperturbed by the presence of multiple involuntary movements (Myslobodsky, 1986; Rosen, Mukherjee, Olarte, Varia, & Cardenas, 1982). Could it be that a lack of insight into their psychotic condition, when present in these patients, has a similar origin? Research has yet to establish any coincidence between lack of insight and unconcern regarding dyskinesia, however, or indeed the presence of any focal lesion.

Where could a focal lesion lie? The similarities between loss of insight and anosognosia might suggest a right parietal lobe lesion such as that said to obtain in anosognostic patients with hemiplegia (Lishman, 1987); this would be consistent with the views of those authors who regard right hemisphere abnormalities as contributing to schizophrenic symptomatology (Cutting, 1985). The role of the right hemisphere in schizophrenia remains a matter of debate, however, and several authors have questioned the focal origins of anosognosia (Weinstein & Cole, 1963; Weinstein & Kahn, 1950, 1955; see Lishman, 1987 for a review).

The nature of the link between schizophrenia and loss of insight does not need to be understood, however, for the importance of insight in determining drug compliance to be recognised and appropriate interventions, perhaps of an educational nature, to be planned. The problem in this regard is that the nature of the link between insight and compliance is complex. The presence of insight does not guarantee compliance: Half of the insightful subjects used by Lin et al. (1979) failed to take their medication. Nor does compliance require insight: 27% of the sample examined by McEvoy et al. (1989) thought that they needed medication although only 13% of them regarded themselves as ill. David (1990) cites the case of a 27-year-old man who sought treatment without believing that he was psychologically unwell.

It may be that such complexities stem from the varying definitions of insight employed by different authors. Aubrey Lewis (1934) was concerned primarily with the ability to re-label morbid phenomena; more recent authors (Gelder, Gath, & Mayou, 1989) have included treatment compliance in their definitions of insight. Research that demonstrates a clear link between insight and compliance tends to include a perceived need for treatment in the definition of insight (Bartko et al., 1988) or to demonstrate a stronger association with compliance in patients who saw a need for treatment than in those who simply regarded themselves as "ill" (Lin et al., 1979; Marder et al., 1983). The suspicion remains, however, that the link between insight and compliance is not consistent. Knowing that one is ill is not the same as knowing that one needs treatment.

The findings reported here would seem to back up this point. Asking patients whether or not they regarded themselves as unwell did not predict whether or not they would comply with treatment. Presumably a number of factors can intervene between recognition of illness and compliance. Some people might regard themselves as unwell but regard treatment as ineffective or are unwilling to put up with side-effects; as pointed out earlier, more qualitative research, examining the decision-making of individual patients, will be required before these issues can be disentangled. What does seem clear is that asking more focused questions, questions relating to whether treatment in the past has helped and whether or not the patient plans to take it in the future, can distinguish likely defaulters from other patients. Even in this respect, however, the complicated nature of the relationship between insight and compliance is apparent. The aspect of insight shown by other authors to bear the closest relationship with compliance, namely, a stated willingness to take medication, increased the likelihood of a patient complying but provided no guarantee of this. An understanding of a patient's views cannot be replaced by one question, however focused.

What are the clinical implications of the finding that a generally optimistic outlook was associated with improved compliance? It is difficult to see how clinicians can, at will, imbue a sense of optimism in their patients. It may be that detailed discussion of continuing care that will be available after the patient leaves the hospital, and of the facilities for the treatment of any relapse should this occur, will render a patient more likely to agree that "whatever happens in the future, I think I will be able to handle it". In this respect, however, the caveat mentioned earlier, that an association is no proof of causation, must be borne in mind. The presence of an association between an optimistic outlook and good compliance provides no guarantee that an intervention designed to increase optimism will make patients more likely to take their prescribed medication.

The clinical implications of illness variables such as delusions and affective change affecting compliance are likely to be even more limited. Treatment is, and will continue to be, aimed at reducing the levels of the symptoms and signs of illness irrespective of the effect on compliance. Further research is required before the association, previously reported, between persecutory delusions and poor compliance can be regarded as a chance finding. It may be that a subset of patients exists whose persecutory delusions pertain to doctors or other health service personnel and that compliance is particularly poor in these patients as a result of their delusions. Again, the issue will be resolved when the issue of compliance is addressed with an emphasis on the phenomenology of schizophrenia and the attitudes of individual patients to their medication and medical supervisors.

Should the fact that the complexity of the treatment regime had no effect on compliance allow clinicians to pay little heed to the number of times per day that patients have to take medication and the number of different drugs that they are receiving? Almost certainly not. It seems much more likely, as discussed earlier, that the subjects' doctors were successfully titrating the complexity of the treatment regimen against a patient's ability to follow it. The same may be true for the absence of an effect of depot, as opposed to oral, phenothiazines. Since the work of

Freeman (1973) there has been a tradition in British psychiatry for patients who have previously exhibited poor compliance to be encouraged to take depot, as opposed to oral, phenothiazines. It may well be that the behaviour of patients who have previously exhibited poor compliance, and who are therefore, as shown here, more likely to comply poorly again, is masking the beneficial effects of depot medication. The research strategy that would best clarify these issues would control for previous compliance and be prospective with a cross-over design.

Akinesia, when present as a side-effect of treatment with phenothiazines, should cause at least as much concern over the likely effect on compliance as other extra-pyramidal symptoms. In addition to the evidence presented here, that it is associated with patients failing to take their treatment, akinesia is usually more easily treated than akathisia, the side-effect that previous research had suggested showed the strongest relationship with failure to take prescribed medication.

Some reasons why patients who have been compulsorily detained may comply poorly with treatment thereafter were suggested in the preceding chapter. They may be rendered antipathetic to treatment by the experience, or the fact that they have been detained may reflect previous poor compliance. The decision as to whether patients should be detained has to depend, however, on whether or not they represent a danger to themselves or other people. It is not clear how considerations relating to compliance could influence such a decision, or indeed whether they should. Insofar as it is possible to draw a conclusion for the clinical practice of psychiatrists, it may be of benefit if the confrontational and stigmatising aspects of compulsory detention are discussed with the patient after his or her mental state has improved and before he or she is discharged. Finally, the results reported here suggest, it may be worthwhile expending extra effort to promote compliance following the first admission of a sufferer from schizophrenia. That previous poor compliance is the best predictor of subsequent poor compliance suggests that, once established, such a pattern is hard to break.

If a consistent theme emerges from the literature review it is that supervision, whether by family members or health service staff, improves compliance. This suggestion is supported, with respect to the influence of members of a patient's family, by the research that has been reported here. It is possible to argue about the mechanism by which supervision may do this. Some would contend that the opportunity for education about the nature and benefits of treatment is the vital ingredient (Falloon, 1984). Others might point to the cajoling influence of close family members (Willcox et al., 1965) or the motivating effect of someone else taking an interest in one's health and welfare (Blackwell,

1976). Whatever the mediating factor, however, the beneficial effects have been reported repeatedly. In addition to the interview-based research that has been advocated here, the time may now be ripe to investigate prospectively the effect on compliance of altering the degree of supervision and support available to people with schizophrenia.

CHAPTER SEVEN

Summary

A review of the literature suggested that people with schizophrenia, like others who attend doctors, frequently fail to comply with treatment. The factors that have been found to be associated with this failure are several. Some are sociodemographic: lower socioeconomic status and low social stability. Others relate to the subject's attitude to his or her treatment: Those who demonstrate impaired insight have been found to comply poorly in contrast to those with a positive, even optimistic attitude to illness and treatment in general and their own condition in particular. Patient education helps, although it is not clear whether the effect is due to the information itself or to the improved level of supervision that often accompanies the information given. Patients are influenced by the attitudes of their doctors and by the nature of medical consultations. Some features of the phenomenology of schizophrenia, namely, delusions and affective change, are, the review suggested, associated with poor compliance. Finally, some features of the treatment that the patient receives have been found to demonstrate the same association. These are the complexity of the treatment regime, the use of oral, as opposed to depot, medication, and the presence of drug side-effects.

The research presented here comprised a two-year prospective study designed to test some of these associations and to examine the effect of some factors that have not been widely studied. The findings, identified in the literature review, which were examined were that patients of low socioeconomic status and low social stability comply poorly, that those with insight and a positive attitude to their predicament comply better, and that some aspects of treatment, namely, a complex drug regime, the use of oral medication (as opposed to depot), and the presence of drug side-effects, are associated with poor adherence. The factors that were examined here, but which have not been widely studied before, were compulsory admission and previous compliance.

Sociodemographic factors had a small effect, which was consistent with that described elsewhere. A patient's insight and attitude were important but in a different way from that described by other authors. Broad measures of insight such as asking the patient "Do you think you have been unwell during this admission?" were poor predictors of compliance. Better were specific questions relating to the patient's perception of previous treatment, "Did treatment help?" and their plans, "Will you take treatment after your discharge?" An optimistic view of the future was also associated with good compliance. The complexity of the drug regime and the use of depot medication showed no such association. This may be because doctors titrate the complexity of a treatment regime against the patient's ability to understand it and use depot phenothiazines to treat those of their patients who have complied poorly with oral medication in the past. Those who experienced side-effects of their medication were less likely to continue taking it but the association was with akinesia, not akathisia as reported by other authors. Patients who had been treated compulsorily complied poorly as did those who had previously ignored the advice of doctors.

Appendix

Attitude scale as developed by Soskis and Bowers (1969).

"Insight positive"
1. When I feel strange or bad I like to stop and figure out what is causing it.
2. It always helps to sit down and think things through.
3. Now that I understand more about myself, I find I can understand other people too and get along better with them.
4. The thing that really counts is understanding why you feel the way you do.
5. Now that I understand why I became ill, I can handle my problems better.

"Insight negative"
1. You'll be healthier if you don't think too much about your problems.
2. You can never really understand your own feelings.
3. There are certain of my problems I would rather forget about.
4. It doesn't really help that much to understand your problems; they keep on coming back anyway.
5. When I feel strange or bad the best thing to do is to keep busy and hope that it will go away.

"Illness positive"
1. I think it made me a better person.
2. Looking back on it now I feel it was best that it happened.
3. In the long run my illness made me better able to handle my problems.
4. In a way my illness helped me grow up.
5. It was a turning point in my life—since then things have got better.

"Illness negative"
1. It's very hard for me to find anything good about my illness.
2. It really should never have happened.
3. All in all, being sick created more problems than it solved.
4. My illness was a big set-back in my life.
5. It was a turning point in my life—since then things have got worse.

"Future positive"
1. Right now the future looks pretty good for me.
2. I think I am up to solving my problems.
3. My future will be better than my past.
4. If I have to go to hospital again I think I will recover.
5. Whatever happens in the future, I think I will be able to handle it.

"Future negative"
1. Right now the future is full of problems.
2. I sometimes wonder if I'll be able to face what the future will bring.
3. My happiest days are in the past.
4. If I have to go to the hospital again, I'm afraid I'll have to stay for a long time.
5. I just don't see how things are going to get any better for me.

References

Altman, H., Angle, H.V., Brown, M.L., & Sletten, I.W. (1972a) Prediction of unauthorised absence. *American Journal of Psychiatry, 128*, 1460–1463.

Altman, H., Brown, M.L., & Sletten, I.W. (1972b) "And ... silently steal away": A study of elopers. *Diseases of the Nervous System, 33*, 52–58.

American Psychiatric Association (1980). *Diagnostic and statistical manual of mental disorders* (3rd edn.). Washington, DC: American Psychiatric Association.

Archer, M., Rinzler, S., & Christakis, G. (1967). Social factors affecting participation in a study of diet and coronary heart disease. *Journal of Health and Social Behaviour, 8*, 22–23.

Baekeland, F., & Lundwall, L. (1975). Dropping out of treatment: A critical review. *Psychological Bulletin, 82*, 735–783.

Baekeland, F., Lundwall, L., and Shanahan, T.J. (1973). Correlates of patient attrition in the outpatient treatment of alcoholism. *Journal of Mental and Nervous Disease, 157*, 99–107.

Bartko, G., Herczeg, I., & Zador, G. (1988). Clinical symptomatology and drug compliance in schizophrenic patients. *Acta Psychiatrica, Scandinavica 77*, 74–76.

Baum, O.E., Felzer, S.B., D'Zmura, T.L., & Shumaker, E. (1966). Psychotherapy, dropouts and lower socioeconomic patients. *American Journal of Orthopsychiatry, 36*, 629–635.

Becker, M.H., Drachman, R.H., & Kirscht, J.P. (1974). A new approach to explaining sick-role behavior in low-income populations. *American Journal of Public Health, 64*, 205–216.

Becker, M.H., Haefner, D.P., Kasl, S.V., Kirscht, J.P., Maiman, L.A., & Rosenstock, I.M. (1977). Selected psychosocial models and correlates of individual health related behaviors. *Medical Care Supplement, 15*, 27–46.

Becker, M.H., & Maiman, L.A. (1975). Sociobehavioral determinants of compliance with health and medical care recommendations. *Medical Care, 13*, 10–24.

Bergman, A.B., & Werner, R.J. (1963). Failure of children to receive penicillin by mouth. *New England Journal of Medicine, 268*, 1334–1338.

Blackwell, B. (1973). Drug therapy: patient compliance. *New England Journal of Medicine, 289*, 249–252.

Blackwell, B. (1976). Treatment adherence. *British Journal of Psychiatry, 129*, 513–531.

Brand, F., Smith, R., & Brand, P. (1977). Effect of economic barriers to medical care on patients' non-compliance. *Public Health Reports, 92*, 72–78.

Brody, E.B., Derbyshire, R.L., & Schliefer, C.B. (1967). How the young adult Baltimore negro male becomes a Maryland hospital statistic. In R.R. Monroe, G.D. Klee and E.B. Brody (Eds.), *Psychiatric Epidemiology and Mental Health Planning, Psychiatric Research Report, Number 22*, (pp.206–219). Washington, DC: American Psychiatric Association.

Brown, J.S., & Kosterlitz, N. (1964). Selection and treatment of psychiatric out-patients. *Archives of General Psychiatry, 11*, 425–438.

Burgoyne, R.W. (1976). Effect of drug ritual changes on schizophrenic patients. *American Journal of Psychiatry, 133*, 284–289.

Bursten, B. (1985). Medication nonadherence due to feelings of loss of control in "biological depression". *American Journal of Psychiatry, 142*, 244–246.

Caine, T.M., & Wijesinghe, B. (1976). Personality, expectancies and group psychotherapy. *British Journal of Psychiatry, 129*, 384–387.

Carr, J.E., & Whittenbaugh, J.A. (1968). Volunteer and nonvolunteer characteristics in an outpatient population. *Journal of Abnormal Psychology, 73*, 16–17.

Cohen, R.L., & Richardson, C.H. (1970). A retrospective study of case attrition in a child psychiatric clinic. *Social Psychiatry, 5*, 77–83.

Cottrell, D., Hill, P., Walk, D., Dearnaley, J., & Ierotheou, A. (1988). Factors influencing non-attendance at child psychiatry out-patient appointments. *British Journal of Psychiatry, 152*, 201–214.

Craig, T.J., & Huffine, C.L. (1976). Correlates of patient attendance in an inner-city mental health clinic. *American Journal of Psychiatry, 133*, 61–65.

Craig, T.J., Huffine, C.L., & Brooks, M. (1974). Completion of referral to psychiatric services by inner-city residents. *Archives of General Psychiatry 31*, 353–357.

Crawford, R., & Forrest, A. (1974). Controlled trial of depot fluphenazine in out-patient schizophrenics. *British Journal of Psychiatry, 124*, 385–391.

Cummings, K.M., Becker, M.H., Kirscht, J.P., & Levin, N.W. (1981). Intervention strategies to improve compliance with medical regimens by ambulatory haemodialysis patients. *Journal of Behavioral Medicine, 4*, 111–127.

Cutting, J.C. (1985). *The psychology of schizophrenia*. Edinburgh: Churchill Livingstone.

David, A.S. (1990). Insight and psychosis. *British Journal of Psychiatry, 157*, 798–808.

Davis, K.L., Estess F.M., Simonton S.C., & Gonda, T.A. (1977). Effects of payment mode on clinic attendance and rehospitalization. *American Journal of Psychiatry, 134*, 576–578.

Davis, M.S. (1966). Variations in patients' compliance with doctors' orders: Analysis of congruence between survey responses and results of empirical observations. *Journal of Medical Education, 41*, 1037–1048.

Davis, M.S. (1967). Predicting non-compliant behavior. *Journal of Health and Social Behaviour, 8*, 265–271.

Davis, M.S. (1968a). Physiologic, psychological and demographic factors in patient compliance with doctors' orders. *Medical Care, 6*, 115–122.

Davis, M.S. (1968b). Variations in patients' compliance with doctors' advice: An experimental analysis of patterns of communication. *American Journal of Public Health, 58*, 274–288.

Dinnen, A. (1971). Change of therapists as a cause of absences from group psychotherapy. *British Journal of Psychiatry, 119*, 625–628.

Dodd, J.A. (1971). A retrospective analysis of variables related to duration of treatment in a university psychiatric clinic. *Journal of Nervous and Mental Disease, 151*, 75–85.

Eisenthal, S., Emery, R., Lazare, A., & Udin, H. (1979). "Adherence" and the negotiated approach to patienthood. *Archives of General Psychiatry, 36*, 393–398.

Evans, L., & Spelman, M. (1983). The problem of non-compliance with drug therapy. *Drugs, 25*, 63–76.

Falloon, I.R.H. (1984). Developing and maintaining adherence to long-term drug-taking regimens. *Schizophrenia Bulletin, 10*, 412–417.

Falloon, I., Watt, D.C., & Shepherd, M. (1978). A comparative controlled trial of pimozide and fluphenazine decanoate in the continuation therapy of schizophrenia. *Psychological Medicine, 8*, 59–70.

Feather, N.T. (1959). Subjective probability and decisions under uncertainty. *Psychological Review, 66*, 150–164.

Fiester, A.R., Mahrer, A.R., Giambra, L.M., & Ormiston, D.W. (1974). Shaping a clinic population: The dropout problem reconsidered. *Community Mental Health Journal, 10*, 173–179.

Folstein, M.F., Folstein, S.E., & McHugh, P.R. (1975). "Mini-mental state". A practical method for grading the cognitive state of patients for the clinician. *Journal of Psychiatric Research, 12*, 189–198.

Francis, V., Korsch, B.M., & Morris, M.J. (1969). Gaps in doctor-patient communication. *New England Journal of Medicine, 280*, 535–540.

Frank, J.D., Gliedman, L.H., Imber, S.D., Nash, E.H., & Stone, A.R. (1957). Why patients leave psychotherapy. *Archives of Neurology and Psychiatry, 77*, 283–299.

Freedman, N., Engelhardt, D.M., Hankoff, L.D., Glick, B.S., Kaye, H., Buchwald, J., & Stark, P. (1958). Dropout from outpatient psychiatric treatment. *Archives of Neurology and Psychiatry, 80*, 657–666.

Freeman, H. (1973). Long-acting neuroleptics and their place in the community mental health services in the United Kingdom. In F.J. Ayd, (Ed.), *The future of pharmacotherapy new drug delivery systems.* (pp.37–42). Baltimore, MD: International Drug Therapy Newsletter.

Geersten, H.R., Gray, R.M., & Ward, J.R. (1973). Patient non-compliance within the context of seeking medical care for arthritis. *Journal of Chronic Disease 26*, 689– 698.

Gelder, M., Gath, D., & Mayou, R. (1989). *The Oxford textbook of psychiatry.* (2nd edn.). Oxford: Oxford University Press.

Gibby, R.G., Stotsky, B.A., Hiler, E.W., & Miller, D.R. (1954). Validation of Rorschach criteria for predicting duration of therapy. *Journal of Consulting Psychology, 18*, 185–191.

Goldberg, S.C., Schooler, N.R., Hogarty, G.E., & Roper, M. (1977). Prediction of relapse in schizophrenic out-patients treated by drug and sociotherapy. *Archives of General Psychiatry, 34*, 171–184.

Gordis, L. (1979). Conceptual and methodological problems in measuring patient compliance. In R.B. Haynes, D.W. Taylor, and D.L. Sackett (Eds.), *Compliance and health care* (pp.23–45). Baltimore, MD: Johns Hopkins University Press.

Gordis, L., Markowitz, M., & Lilienfeld, A.M. (1969). The inaccuracy in using interviews to estimate patient reliability in taking medications at home. *Medical Care, 7*, 49–54.

Gordon, H.L., & Groth, C. (1961). Mental patients wanting to stay in the hospital. *Archives of General Psychiatry, 4*, 124–130.

Gould, M.S., Shaffer, D., & Kaplan, D. (1985). The characteristics of dropouts from a child psychiatry clinic. *Journal of the American Academy of Child Psychiatry, 24*, 316–328.

Gray, R.M., Kesler, J.P., & Moody, P.M. (1966). Effects of social class and friends' expectations on oral polio vaccination participation. *American Journal of Public Health, 56*, 2028–2032.

Greenwald, A.F., & Bartemeier, L.H. (1963). Psychiatric discharges against medical advice. *Archives of General Psychiatry, 8*, 117–119.

Hagan, L.D., Beck, N.C., Kunce, J.T., & Heiser, G.H. (1983). Facilitating psychiatric patient follow-up: A study of transfer attrition. *Journal of Clinical Psychology, 39*, 494–498.

Hardy, M.C. (1948). Follow-up of medical recommendations. *Journal of the American Medical Association, 136*, 20–27.

Hare, E.H., & Willcox, D.R.C. (1967). Do psychiatric inpatients take their pills? *British Journal of Psychiatry, 113*, 1435–1439.

Havens, L.L. (1968). Some difficulties in giving schizophrenic and borderline patients medication. *Psychiatry, 31*, 44–50.

Haynes, R.B. (1979). Determinants of compliance: The disease and the mechanics of treatment. In R.B. Haynes, D.W. Taylor, and D.L. Sackett (Eds.), *Compliance in health care*, (pp.49–62). Baltimore, MD: Johns Hopkins University Press.

Haynes, R.B., Taylor, D.W., & Sackett, D.L. (Eds.) (1979). *Compliance in health care*. Baltimore, MD: Johns Hopkins University Press.

Heinrichs, D.W., Cohen, B.P., & Carpenter, W.T. (1985). Early insight and the management of schizophrenic decompensation. *Journal of Nervous and Mental Disease, 173*, 133–138.

Heinzelmann, F., & Bagley, R.W. (1970). Response to physical activity programs and their effects on health behavior. *Public Health Reports, 85*, 905–911.

Hertz, C.G., Bernheim, J.W., & Perloff, T.N. (1976). Patient participation in the problem-oriented system: A health care plan. *Medical Care, 14*, 77–79.

Hiler, E.W. (1959). Initial complaints as predictors of continuation in psychotherapy. *Journal of Clinical Psychology, 15*, 344–345.

Hogan, T.P., Awad, A.G., & Eastwood, R. (1983). A self-report scale predictive of drug compliance in schizophrenics: Reliability and descriminative validity. *Psychological Medicine, 13*, 177–183.

Howard, K., Rickels, K., Mock, J.E., Lipman, R.S., Covi, L., & Bauman, N.C. (1970). Therapeutic style and attrition rate from psychiatric drug treatment. *Journal of Nervous and Mental Disease, 150*, 102–110.

Hulka, B., Cassel, J., Kupper, L., & Burdette, J. (1976). Communication, compliance and concordance between physicians and patients with prescribed medications. *American Journal of Public Health, 66*, 847–853.

Hurtado, A., Greenlick, M., & Columbo, T. (1973). Determinants of medical care utilisation: Failure to keep appointments. *Medical Care, 11*, 189–198.

Inui, T.S., Yourtee, E.L., & Williamson, J.W. (1976). Improved outcomes in hypertension after physician tutorials: A controlled trial. *Annals of Internal Medicine, 84*, 646– 651.

Irwin, D.S., Weitzel, W.D., & Morgan, D.W. (1971). Phenothiazine intake and staff attitudes. *American Journal of Psychiatry, 127*, 1631–1635.

Johnson, D.A.W. (1974). A study of the use of anti-depressant medication in general practice. *British Journal of Psychiatry, 125*, 186–192.

Johnson, D.A.W. (1977). Practical considerations in the use of depot neuroleptics for the treatment of schizophrenia. *British Journal of Hospital Medicine, 17*, 546–558.

Johnson, D.A.W., & Freeman, H. (1972). Long-acting tranquillisers. *Practitioner, 208*, 395–400.

Johnson, D.A.W., & Freeman, H. (1973). Drug defaulting by patients on long-acting phenothiazines. *Psychological Medicine, 3*, 115–119.

Joyce, C.R.B., Caple, G., Mason, M., Reynolds, E., & Mathews, J.A. (1969). Quantitative study of doctor-patient communication. *Quarterly Journal of Medicine, 38*, 183–194.

Kanzler, M., Jaffe, J., & Zeidenberg, P. (1976). Long- and short-term effectiveness of a large-scale proprietary smoking cessation programme—a four-year follow-up of Smokenders participants. *Journal of Clinical Psychology, 32*, 661– 669.

Katz, J., & Solomon, R.Z. (1958). The patient and his experiences in an out-patient clinic. *Archives of Neurology and Psychiatry, 80*, 86–92.

Korsch, B.M., & Negrete, V.F. (1972). Doctor-patient communication. *Scientific American, 227*, 66–74.

Lefebvre, A., Sommerauer, J., Cohen, N., Waldron, S., & Perry, I. (1983). Where did all the "no-shows" go? *Canadian Journal of Psychiatry, 28*, 387–390.

Leventhal, H. (1971). Fear appeals and persuasion: The differentiation of a motivational construct. *American Journal of Public Health, 61*, 1208–1224.

Lewis, A. (1934). The psychopathology of insight. *British Journal of Medical Psychology, 14*, 332–348.

Lewis, W.C., Lorenz, T.H., & Calden, G. (1955). Irregular discharge from tuberculosis hospitals. *Psychosomatic Medicine, 17*, 276–289.

Ley, P., & Morris, L. (1984). Psychological aspects of written information for patients. In S. Rachman (Ed.), *Contributions to medical psychology*, Vol.1, (pp.117–149). Oxford: Pergamon Press

Ley, P., & Spelman, M.S. (1965). Communications in an out-patient setting. *British Journal of Social and Clinical Psychology, 4*, 114–116.

Lin, I.F., Spiga, R., & Fortsch, W. (1979). Insight and adherence to medication in chronic schizophrenics. *Journal of Clinical Psychiatry, 40*, 430–432.

Lipman, R.S., Rickels, K., Uhlenhuth, E.H., Park, L.C., & Fisher, S. (1965). Neurotics who fail to take their drugs. *British Journal of Psychiatry, 111*, 1043–1049.

Lishman, W.A. (1987). *Organic psychiatry: The psychological consequences of cerebral disorder* (2nd edn.). Oxford: Blackwell.

Lowinger, P., & Dobie, S. (1968). The attitudes of the psychiatrist about his patient. *Comprehensive Psychiatry, 9*, 627–632.

Marder, S.R., Mebane, A., Chien, C.P., Winslade, W.J., Swann, E., & Van Putten, T. (1983). A comparison of patients who refuse and consent to neuroleptic treatment. *American Journal of Psychiatry, 140*, 470–472.

Mayer, J. (1972). Initial alcoholism clinic attendance of patients with legal referrals. *Quarterly Journal of Studies on Alcohol, 33*, 814–816.

Mazzullo, J.V., Lasagna, L., & Grinar, P.F. (1974). Variations in interpretation of clinic instructions: The need for improved prescribing habits. *Journal of the American Medical Association, 227*, 929–931.

McEvoy, J.P., Apperson, L.J., Appelbaum, P.S., Ortlip, P., Brecosky, J., Hammill, K., Geller, J.L., & Roth, L. (1989). Insight in schizophrenia. Its relationship to acute psychopathology. *Journal of Nervous and Mental Disease, 177*, 43–47.

McGlashan, T.H., & Carpenter, W.T. (1981). Does attitude toward psychosis relate to outcome? *American Journal of Psychiatry, 138*, 797–801.

Mechanic, D., & Volkart, E.H. (1961). Stress, illness behavior and the sick role. *American Sociological Review, 26*, 51–58.

Meichenbaum, D., & Turk, D. (1987). *Facilitating treatment adherence: A practitioner's guidebook.* New York: Plenum.

Michaux, W.W. (1961). Side effects, resistance and dosage deviations in psychiatric outpatients treated with tranquillizers. *Journal of Nervous and Mental Disease, 133*, 203–212.

Morisky, D.E., Green, L.W., & Levine, D.M. (1986). Concurrent and predictive validity of a self-reported measure of medication adherence. *Medical Care 24*, 67–74.

Mozdzierz, G.J., Macchitelli, F.J., Conway, J.A., & Krauss, H.H. (1973). Personality characteristic differences between alcoholics who leave treatment against medical advice and those who don't. *Journal of Clinical Psychology, 29*, 78–82.

Muller, D.J. (1962). The "missing" patient. *British Medical Journal, 1*, 177–179.

Myers, E.D. (1975). Age, persistence and improvement in an out-patient group. *British Journal of Psychiatry, 127*, 157–159.

Myslobodsky, M.S. (1986). Anosognosia in tardive dyskinesia: A symptom of "tardive dysmentia" or "tardive dementia". *Schizophrenia Bulletin, 12*, 1–6.

Nelson, A. (1975). Drug default among schizophrenic patients. *American Journal of Hospital Pharmacy, 32*, 1237–1242.

Nelson, P.C., & Hoffmann, H. (1972). Personalities of alcoholics who leave and seek treatment. *Psychological Reports, 30*, 949–950.

Nikias, M.K. (1968). Social class and the use of dental care under prepayment. *Medical Care, 6*, 381–393.

Novick, J., Benson, R., & Rembar, J. (1981). Patterns of termination in an out-patient clinic for children and adolescents. *Journal of the American Academy of Child Psychiatry, 20*, 834–844.

Orford, J. (1974). Simplistic thinking about other people as a predictor of early dropout at an alcoholism halfway house. *British Journal of Medical Psychology, 47*, 53–62.

Overall, J.E., & Gorham, D.R. (1962). The brief psychiatric rating scale. *Psychological Reports, 10*, 799–812.

Park, L.C., & Lipman, R.S. (1964). A comparison of patient dosage deviation reports with pill counts. *Psychopharmacologia, 6*, 299–302.

Parkes, C.M., Brown, G.W., & Monck, E.M. (1962). The general practitioner and the schizophrenic patient. *British Medical Journal, 1*, 972–976.

Parkin, D.M., Henney, C.R., Quirk, J., & Crooks, J. (1976). Deviation from prescribed drug treatment after discharge from hospital. *British Medical Journal, 2*, 686–687.

Parsons T. (1982). *On institutions and social evolution.* University of Chicago Press.

Perkins, M.E., & Bloch, H.I. (1971). A study of some failures in methadone treatment. *American Journal of Psychiatry, 126*, 1389–1396.

Pisani, V.D., & Motansky, G.U. (1970). Predictors of premature termination of outpatient followup group psychotherapy among male alcoholics. *International Journal of Addictions, 5*, 731–737.

Porter, A.M.W. (1969). Drug defaulting in general practice. *British Medical Journal, 1*, 218–222.

Pragoff, H. (1962). Adjustment of tuberculosis patients one year after hospital discharge. *Public Health Reports, 77*, 671–679.

Prickman, L.E., Koelsche, G.A., Berkman, J.M., Carryer, H.M., Peters, G.A., & Henderson, L.L. (1958). Does the executive health program meet its objective? *Journal of the American Medical Association, 167*, 1451–1455.

Prien, R.F., & Caffey, E.M. (1977). Long-term maintenance drug therapy in recurrent affective illness: Current status and issues. *Diseases of the Nervous System, 38*, 981–992.

Quinn, R., Federspiel, C., Lefkowitz, L., & Christie, A. (1977). Recurrences and sequelae of rheumatic fever in Nashville. *Journal of the American Medical Association, 238*, 1512–1515.

Rae, J.B. (1972). The influence of the wives on the treatment outcome of alcoholics: A follow-up study of two years. *British Journal of Psychiatry, 120*, 601–613.

Raynes, A.E., & Patch, V.D. (1971). Distinguishing features of patients who discharge themselves from a psychiatric ward. *Comprehensive Psychiatry, 12*, 473–479.

Renton, C.A., Affleck, J.W., Carstairs, G.M., & Forrest, A.D. (1963). A follow-up of schizophrenic patients in Edinburgh. *Acta Psychiatrica Scandinavica, 39,* 548–581.

Reynolds, E., Joyce, C.R.B., Swift, J.L., Tooley, P.H., & Weatherall, M. (1965). Psychological and clinical investigation of the treatment of anxious out-patients with three barbiturates and placebo. *British Journal of Psychiatry, 111,* 84–95.

Richards, A.D. (1964). Attitude and drug acceptance. *British Journal of Psychiatry, 110,* 46–52.

Ried, L.D., & Christensen, D.B. (1988). A psychosocial perspective in the explanation of patients' drug-taking behaviour. *Social Science and Medicine, 27,* 277–289.

Rockart, J.F., & Hofmann, P.B. (1969). Physician and patient behavior under different scheduling systems in a hospital outpatient department. *Medical Care, 7,* 463– 470.

Rosen, A.M., Mukherjee, S., Olarte, S., Varia, V., & Cardenas, C. (1982). Perception of tardive dyskinesia in outpatients receiving maintenance neuroleptics. *American Journal of Psychiatry, 139,* 372–373.

Rosenberg, C.M. (1974). Drug maintenance in the out-patient treatment of chronic alcoholism. *Archives of General Psychiatry, 30,* 373–377.

Rosenberg, C.M., Davidson, G.E., & Patch, V.D. (1972). Drop-outs from a methadone program for addicts. *International Journal of Addictions, 7,* 415–425.

Rosenstock, I.M. (1966). Why people use health services. *Milbank Memorial Fund Quarterly, 44,* 94–127.

Ross, A.O., & Lacey, H.M. (1961). Characteristics of terminators and remainers in child guidance treatment. *Journal of Consulting Psychology, 25,* 420–424.

Royal Statistical Society (1986). *The GLIM System, Release 3.77.* Oxford: Numerical Algorithms Group.

Sackett, D.L., Haynes, R.B., Gibson, E.S., Hackett, B.C., Wayne Taylor, D., Roberts, R.S., & Johnson, A.L. (1975). Randomised clinical trial of strategies for improving medication compliance in primary hypertension. *Lancet, 1,* 1205–1207.

Schou, M., Baastrup, P.C., Grof, P., Weis, P., & Angst, J. (1970). Pharmacological and clinical problems of lithium prophylaxis. *British Journal of Psychiatry, 116,* 615–619.

Schulman, B.A. (1979). Active patient orientation and outcomes in hypertension treatment. *Medical Care, 17,* 267–280.

Schwartz, D., Wang, M., Zeitz, L., & Goss, M.E. (1962). Medication errors made by elderly, chronically ill patients. *American Journal of Public Health, 52,* 2018–2029.

Seeman, M.V. (1974). Patients who abandon psychotherapy: Why and when. *Archives of General Psychiatry, 30,* 486–491.

Sheiner, L.B., Rosenberg, B.R., Marathe, V.V., & Peck, C. (1974). Difference in serum digoxin concentrations between outpatients and inpatients: An effect of compliance. *Clinical Pharmacology and Therapeutics, 15,* 239–246.

Soskis, D.A. (1978). Schizophrenic and medical in-patients as informed drug consumers. *Archives of General Psychiatry, 35,* 645–649.

Soskis, D.A., & Bowers, M.B. (1969). The schizophrenic experience. *Journal of Nervous and Mental Disease, 149,* 443–449.

Spitzer, R.L., Endicott, J., Gibson, M., & Robins, E. (1978). Research diagnostic criteria: Rationale and reliability. *Archives of General Psychiatry, 35,* 773– 782.

Stimson, G.V. (1974). Obeying doctors' orders: A view from the other side. *Social Science and Medicine, 8,* 97–104.

Suchman, E.A. (1967). Preventive health behavior: A model for research on community health campaigns. *Journal of Health and Social Behavior, 8,* 197–209.

Turner, R.J., Gardner, E.A., & Higgins, A.C. (1970). Epidemiological data for mental health centre planning. 1. Field survey methods in psychiatry: The problem of the lost population. *American Journal of Public Health, 60,* 1040–1051.

Vaisrub, S. (1975). You can lead a horse to water. *Journal of the American Medical Association, 234,* 80–81.

Van Putten, T. (1974). Why do schizophrenic patients refuse to take their drugs? *Archives of General Psychiatry, 31,* 67–72.

Van Putten, T., Crumpton E., & Yale, C. (1976). Drug refusal in schizophrenia and the wish to be crazy. *Archives of General Psychiatry, 33,* 1443–1445.

Vaughn, C., & Leff, J.P. (1976). The influence of family and social factors on the course of psychiatric illness. *British Journal of Psychiatry, 129,* 125–137.

Voth, A.C. (1965). Autokinesis and alcoholism. *Quarterly Journal of Studies on Alcohol, 26,* 412–422.

Waters, W.H., Gould, N.V., & Lunn, J.E. (1976). Undispensed prescriptions in a mining general practice. *British Medical Journal, 1,* 1062–1063.

Weinstein, E.A., & Cole, M. (1950). The syndrome of anosognosia. *Archives of Neurology and Psychiatry, 64,* 772–791.

Weinstein, E.A., & Kahn, R.L. (1955). *Denial of illness: Symbolic and physiological aspects.* Springfield, IL: Charles Thomas.

Weinstein, E.A., & Kahn, R.L. (1963). Concepts of anosognosia. In L. Halpern (Ed.), *Problems of dynamic neurology* (pp.254–273). Jerusalem: Hadassah Medical School.

West, D., Graham, S., Swanson, M., & Wilkinson, G. (1977). Five year follow-up of a smoking withdrawal clinic population. *American Journal of Public Health, 67,* 536– 544.

Wheatley, D. (1968). Effects of doctors' and patients' attitudes and other factors on response to drugs. In K. Rickels (Ed.), *Non-specific factors in drug therapy* (pp.73–79). Springfield, IL: Charles Thomas

Wilkinson, A.E., Prado, W.M., Williams, W.O., & Schnadt, F.W. (1971). Psychological test characteristics and length of stay in alcoholism treatment. *Quarterly Journal of Studies on Alcohol, 32*, 60–65.

Willcox, D.R., Gillan, R., & Hare, E.H. (1965). Do psychiatric out-patients take their drugs? *British Medical Journal, 2*, 790–792.

Wilson, J.D., & Enoch, M.D. (1967). Estimation of drug rejection by schizophrenic in-patients, with analysis of clinical factors. *British Journal of Psychiatry, 113*, 209–211.

Winder, A.E., & Hersko, M. (1955). The effect of social class on the length and type of psychotherapy in a Veterans Administration mental hygiene clinic. *Journal of Clinical Psychology, 11*, 77–79.

Winkelman, N.W. (1964). A clinical and socio-cultural study of 200 psychiatric patients started on chlorpromazine 10.5 years ago. *American Journal of Psychiatry, 120*, 861–869.

Wooley, S.C., & Blackwell, B. (1975). A behavioral probe into social contingencies on a psychosomatic ward. *Journal of Applied Behavioral Analysis, 8*, 337–339.

World Health Organisation (1973) *Report of the International Pilot Study of Schizophrenia,* Vol. 1. Geneva: World Health Organisation.

Author index

Subject index

FORTHCOMING MONOGRAPHS

AGGRESSION, INDIVIDUAL DIFFERENCES, ALCOHOL AND BENZODIAZEPINES

Alyson Bond, Malcolm Lader, José Carlos C. da Silveira

THE RAPIST

Donald Grubin and John Gunn

THE DRUG TRANSITION STUDIES

Changes in Route of Administration of Heroin and Cocaine for Populations and Individuals

John Strang, Michael Gossop

PSYCHOSIS IN THE INNER CITY

David Castle, Simon Wessely, Jim Van Os, Robin Murray

For more information, please contact:

The Promotions Department
Psychology Press
27 Church Road, Hove
East Sussex, (UK) BN3 2FA
Tel: +44 (0) 1273 207 411   Fax: +44 (0) 1273 205 612

———